**Neel Shah** is an experienced sports ICF-certified life coach, educator and over two decades on the developme: sport in North America, Asia and Europe. In 2018, he established the Global Institute of Sports Business. Here, he currently serves as the associate dean and the head of counselling.

Prior to setting up the institute with India On Track, Neel was the CEO of DSK Shivajians FC and the Liverpool FC International Academy-DSK. Before stepping into professional club management, he served as the business director for Libero Sports. Preceding his move to India in 2009, Neel spent seven years with New York-based Major League Soccer serving as director of fan development.

Shah received his bachelor's degree in Business Economics with an emphasis in Sports Management from the University of California, Santa Barbara, and a certificate in Economics from University College London. He secured his MBA in Sports Management from Seton Hall University.

Shah is a regular TEDx speaker and serves as visiting faculty and guest lecturer at several universities. He is also an avid practitioner of mindfulness, meditation and yoga.

# YOUR DREAM CAREER

## How to Choose the One That Fulfils You

**NEEL SHAH**

Om Books International

First published in 2023 by

## Om Books International

**Corporate and Editorial Office**
A-12, Sector 64, Noida 201 301
Uttar Pradesh, India
Phone: +91 120 477 4100
Email: editorial@ombooks.com
Website: www.ombooksinternational.com

**Sales Office**
107, Ansari Road, Darya Ganj,
New Delhi 110 002, India
Phone: +91 11 4000 9000
Email: sales@ombooks.com
Website: www.ombooks.com

ISBN: 978-93-5376-856-0

Printed in India

10 9 8 7 6 5 4 3 2 1

*To*
*Mom and Dad,*
*thanks for always creating space*
*for me to discover and live my dream*

'Your time is limited, so don't waste it living someone else's life …'

# Contents

Foreword                                                                    ix
Preface                                                                      xi

1. **Show Me the Money**                                                      1
   *Don't We Work to Make Money?*

2. **The Magic Elements for Career Fulfilment**                               5
   *How Does Being Unfulfilled at Work Affect Your Life?*

3. **Pursue Your Passion**                                                   11
   *What Are You Deeply Interested in?*

4. **Tap into Your Superpower**                                              23
   *What Are You Extraordinary at?*

5. **Live Your Purpose in Life**                                             35
   *How Do You Want to Contribute to the World?*

6. **Perfect Your Mission Statement**                                        42
   *How Do You Make Your Words Your World?*

7. **How I Landed My Dream Job**                                             55
   *Is It Possible to Make Your Dream a Reality?*

8. **The Method to Kick-start Your Dream Career**  67
   *How to Figure Out Your Dream Job(s)?*

9. **The Dream Jobs Process Proved Successful**  81
   *How Does This Work in Real Life?*

10. **My Giant Leap Forward**  92
    *What Happens When Your Dream Job Is No Longer a Dream?*

11. **Potential Pitfalls Become a Thing of the Past**  110
    *But What If You Are Still Not Convinced?*

12. **Learn the Rules of the Game to Play It Well**  120
    *How Do You Remain on Your Dream Career Path?*

13. **Professional Fulfilment Matters**  132
    *What Is Really Important in Your Career?*

14. **The Steps I Took to Design My Dream Career**  140
    *How the Process Can Help You Enjoy a Fulfilling Career?*

15. **Overcome Your Inner Demons**  151
    *Why Are You Not Able to Move Forward?*

16. **Find Your Career Bliss**  162
    *Are You Worthy of a Career That Will Bring You Fulfilment?*

17. **Begin Your Dream Career Journey**  170
    *Are You Ready?*

*Acknowledgements*  174

# Foreword

I have been fortunate enough to come across many inspiring individuals throughout my career in sports journalism and broadcasting. People who through their work push others to pursue their dreams and find fulfilment in their professional lives. Neel Shah is one of those individuals, and this book is a testament to his passion for helping others understand the importance of professional fulfilment.

In *Your Dream Career*, Neel provides a comprehensive and accessible guide for anyone seeking to unlock their true potential and find lasting satisfaction in their chosen field. The book is a valuable resource that not only highlights the significance of pursuing our dreams but also offers practical steps to achieve them. Neel's dedication in crafting this guide must be commended, as he expertly combines wisdom, insights, and actionable advice to empower his readers.

It reminded me of the choices I made as a South Asian growing up in Leicester, England. The traditional career pathways of becoming a doctor, engineer or lawyer often stood as the default choices in my community. However, I dared to follow my heart, deviating from those well-trodden paths, and ventured into the world of radio and television. This decision, which some may have deemed unconventional, has shaped my life in immeasurable ways, leading to deep career fulfilment over the past twenty-five years.

By pursuing my passion for broadcasting and immersing myself in the world of sport, I have experienced a sense of purpose that transcends the confines of a 'normal job'. Each week, I have the incredible opportunity to tap into my passion and share the beautiful game of football with over 700 million viewers globally, and the profound impact that aligning with our purpose can have on every aspect of our lives.

Neel's book opens our eyes to the significance of creating a dream career. I genuinely believe that when we find ourselves in professions that resonate with our passion, we unlock our true potential and radiate positive energy in all we do. I hope those who read this book will be inspired to embark on their own transformative journeys, armed with the wisdom and guidance provided in these pages.

Ultimately, we as individuals hold immense power to shape our destinies. *Your Dream Career* serves as a roadmap for those seeking to navigate the often complex terrain of professional fulfilment. I encourage you to dive into its pages with an open mind and a heart full of ambition. Allow this book to be your guide as you chart your own course towards a career that embodies your passion, harnesses your unique abilities and fulfils your deepest aspirations.

Congratulations to Neel on his publication. One which will undoubtedly inspire countless individuals to embrace the journey of creating their dream careers. May this book serve as a catalyst for transformation, leading to a world where people find joy and purpose in their chosen paths.

**Manish Bhasin**
Sports journalist and presenter

# Preface

'Imagine you are in your dream job.'

I clearly remember sitting in my fifth-grade classroom and our teacher, Mrs Shea, asking us to close our eyes and envision that we are adults and in our dream job. To picture what we would be working on, who our colleagues would be and what our office environment would look like. To visualize how it felt to be getting paid for doing something that we love. At the time, we only knew about a few interesting professions, so most of my classmates pictured themselves in one of the following jobs: professional athlete, actor/actress, firefighter, police officer, pilot or teacher.

It is quite funny that to most ten-year-olds, the whole job market primarily comprises of individuals who entertain, protect, transport or educate people. I chose to be an actor, but that is beside the point. When I think back to that simple exercise, what sticks out in my memory is having this strong feeling that no matter what job I ended up doing as an adult, that I must enjoy it. I remember when I thought about getting paid to do something I love, it put a smile on my face.

It seems so simple, right? Getting paid to do something you love.

Pursuing work in a field that makes you happy is anything but simple. What most ten-year-olds do not realize is that in just five years, they will study a plethora of subjects to prepare for careers they do not fully understand. That people who love them will be asking questions about their future plans and pushing them in different directions, which will further confuse them. All before they have adequately developed a sense of who they are and where they want to go.

This is what I went through, and I am confident that this is the experience of many readers of this book. It is shocking how quickly we all go from being carefree children to anxious teenagers pressured to make decisions that could impact the rest of our lives. Fortunately, I am one of the people who was lucky enough to 'wake up' during the mad rush to plan my future and end up pursuing professions that genuinely made me happy. And I found out how to always get paid to do something I enjoy.

I am an International Coaching Federation (ICF) certified professional coach specializing in career counselling. I do not have a doctorate in behavioural or organizational psychology. I have average looks, average height, average intelligence, and I grew up in an upper-middle-class family who lived in a one-storey home on a cul-de-sac located in American suburbia. Okay, maybe above average looks … And I am not the CEO of a Fortune 500 company, who has earned millions of dollars. *Not yet.*

So, you must be wondering what gives me the confidence to share my story and offer some career guidance to you.

Well, my life's journey has generated some unique wisdom and insights into how to enjoy a dream career and nearly every person I have worked with has benefitted from them. I am just an ordinary person who has had the good fortune to live an extraordinary professional life.

I genuinely believe that this book will help people create fulfilling careers, leading to happier lives.

I feel enlivened when I speak to someone who loves their work. Typically, their energy levels are high. And just like me, they feel blessed that they have created a career that is in line with who they are and with the kind of service they would like to offer the world. I always leave these conversations feeling light and upbeat.

Happy people=Happy world

*Who would not like to live in a world full of happy people?*

Yet, no matter which continent I am on, more often than not, I come across people who are dealing with some version of the following professional challenges:

- They are young and have no idea of what they want to do professionally.
- They have a sense of what they want to do but feel stuck in their current role.
- They are not fulfilled by their current jobs, are not sure of what they want to do professionally and have resigned themselves into believing that 'this is life'.

*Are you one of them?*

These were painful conversations because I had no understanding or clarity of how I could support these individuals beyond being a good listener.

Why are some of us fortunate enough to enjoy our jobs, and others survive or loathe them?

It is questions like this that led me to develop techniques to support anyone looking to achieve professional fulfilment in their lives.

Over the past twenty years, my jobs have been fulfilling, impactful and natural extensions of myself. I have coached individuals who took steps to pursue vocations that are natural extensions of themselves instead of suffering in unsatisfying jobs. I believe in the truth derived from direct experience. Hence, I have included many anecdotes in this book from my rather eventful life. Reading it will give you the fantastic opportunity to integrate into your life the unique principles and practices I have developed over the years.

My book is honest, straightforward and offers an easy-to-implement process that will allow you to ensure that you are always on the path of professional fulfilment. It will make you think, reflect, dream and motivate you to take the necessary steps to get you out of your comfort zone and on to a professional pathway aligned with your authentic self. You will realize that planning a career is an exciting adventure into the unknown instead of a dispiriting journey down a bumpy road.

'When you want something, all the universe conspires in helping you achieve it.' — Paulo Coelho

He could not have been more right. The universe does look after those who dare to follow their heart, no matter how scary it may seem.

I feel blessed and grateful for my journey and I know that with the right approach, anyone can experience professional fulfilment by creating a career path that leaves them feeling alive and empowered.

The chapters are built upon the premise that professional fulfilment is possible when your careers are a natural extension of yourself. I have intentionally used the word 'careers' instead of 'career' as I feel that it is more relevant in the modern world. The days when someone would graduate from a university, join a company and move up the corporate ladder for the next forty-five years until retirement is no longer the norm. I do not intend to knock any company 'lifers' as I have tremendous respect for those who commit their lives to serve a single organization or industry. However, humans are dynamic beings. To remain motivated in and fulfilled by your professional activities, changing your career may be required—something that I will dive deeper into later in this book.

What I mean by 'a natural extension of yourself' is that it is possible for work not to feel like work.

*Is that even possible?*

The answer is a resounding yes!

You will experience this when what you do is aligned with who you are, not necessarily what you *think* you want. But for this to be attainable, you need to have a sense of who you are— the real you as opposed to the self which can be influenced by internal and external forces such as ego, expectations, family pressures, societal norms and religious dogma. Self-knowledge is the essence of human maturity. It is your greatest responsibility, the task to which you must devote time and effort. And this is not an ability you can acquire overnight. In fact, it is an ongoing adventure that lasts a lifetime *because you change over time.*

Thus, there is no one 'dream job', which often turns out to be anything but a dream in the long run. This is like looking for specific superficial qualities in a 'dream partner' and then being attached to those qualities forever regardless of how you evolve as an individual. Hence, I do not believe in a dream job; *I believe in dream jobs* because you change over time—you mature, evolve and move forward. So, as I see and have lived it, a dream career is essentially a fulfilled professional journey which positively impacts all aspects of one's experience of life.

How do you know if a dream career is feasible or just a pipe dream?

*Read this book.*

Read it with an open heart and mind, and understand that securing a dream career involves self-reflection and a willingness to take focused steps to create a self-aligned career pathway. This book will provide you with the skills, clarity and inspiration you need to ensure a fulfilled, impactful and successful professional life.

# 1

## Show Me the Money

*Don't We Work to Make Money?*

### When I Had Nothing to Offer to the World except My Own Confusion

'*Beta*, get good grades and pursue a career in a field that pays well, so that you can earn a lot of money and provide for your family.'

From the age of ten to twenty, this was the clear and consistent career advice offered by the Indian uncles and aunties in our community. (Desis have this quirk of calling unrelated people 'uncles' and 'aunties' who are always willing to offer free advice.)

I grew up in beautiful Orange County, California, in the 1980s and 90s. The son of two hard-working Indian immigrants who moved to the United States from Gujarat in the late 1960s. You could say that I was a typical A-B-C-D-E-F-G or American-born confused desi emigrated from Gujarat. While pursuing my MBA at Seton Hall University, New Jersey, I became A-B-

C-D-E-F-G-H-I-J or American-born confused desi emigrated from Gujarat home in Jersey.

Throughout my childhood and adolescent years, I was simultaneously living as a part of two different cultures and completely confused about many things especially about how to build a successful life. While the conversation at home and Indian functions focused around study, hard work and earning a lot of money, outside of the immigrant community, the conversation was often along these lines, 'Follow your heart and do whatever you want as long as *you make a lot of money*.' Honestly, at the time, I did not have a clue what 'a lot of money' actually looked like, but I just knew I needed to have it …

## Learning the Hard Way

My friends and I used to spend our summers at Wild Rivers, our local water park. We just loved the place. We would get to the park early and bounce around the entire day zipping down the nearly vertical slides plummeting into the pool below. Then body-surf in the wave pool followed by hours of floating along the lazy river without a care in the world. During one of our gluttonous lunches at the water park, I saw a post on the bulletin board saying that they were looking for someone to fill a lifeguard position.

Jackpot!

This was my opportunity to get paid to do what I wanted, which, at the time, was to hang out at Wild Rivers all day. I decided to start earning money. I applied, got the job and within less than a fortnight, I was standing in the children's pool wearing my bright red shorts, sporting a matching red whistle, à la *Baywatch* style, fully prepared to save anyone who may happen to drown in the three feet of water that filled the pool. It only took my first shift to realize there was a massive difference in my experience when it came to being an employee of Wild Rivers versus being a guest. I gracefully resigned by my third shift, happily returned my whistle and went back to riding slides instead of 'saving lives'.

Breakdown? No, *breakthrough*!

I may not have saved anyone but the experience *saved* me by teaching me an invaluable lesson: While something may seem 'cool' to do as a job, career, or profession, this sentiment may change the second you realize that you will be doing this every day for eight to ten hours a day.

This was a hard-hitting lesson, as up until that point, I had envied lifeguards, Disneyland employees or people who worked at ski lodges, basically anyone who worked at a place I loved to frequent as a guest. My naive teenage self had always assumed that if the place was fun, then working there daily must also be fun. However, I quickly understood this was not a sure-fire formula. It did not mean that these were not good jobs; it just meant that there was no guarantee that I would enjoy the job simply because I liked the ambience it offered.

The Wild Rivers fiasco left me with a bit of a problem: I still wanted to earn money but did not want to loathe going to work each day. Also, if I resigned from a second consecutive job, I would lose face in front of my father, who was known for his resiliency despite many personal and professional challenges. So I decided to just focus on making money regardless of whether I liked the job or not. This led me to summers serving food at Geppetto's Pizzeria, managing the footwear department at Sports Chalet and running around as a floor employee at an Old Navy clothing store. None of these roles was my dream job, but they provided me with an opportunity to learn, make some money on the side and gain clarity on what I did *not* want to do.

## Is Optimism in This Age a Revolutionary Act?

Spending my late teens and early twenties working across so many industries gave me a perspective about the importance of pursuing a career that you enjoy versus landing a job to pay the bills. Money was essential, and thanks to those jobs, I could have some extra cash to pay for my daily expenses. However, to be honest, I struggled during many of those long days and often wondered what was the point of so much education, just to do a job that is not fulfilling and does not allow me to properly utilize my strengths. This led to the obvious question: How to pursue a job that you love?

The challenge was that whenever I brought this up, most people around me would quash my curiosity and optimism by saying, 'This idea of loving your job is not a real thing', or 'If everyone went for jobs they loved, then there would be no one to wash windows or cut grass or work at fast-food restaurants'. Back then and even now, this seemed like a defeatist attitude, which, to me, is no different from saying, 'What's the point of doing anything, we are going to die anyway?' This may seem extreme; however, I believe that intentionally choosing a career pathway that is not aligned with who you are and how you would like to serve the world is, in a way, a sort of slow death in itself.

> 'If the ladder is not leaning against the right wall, every step we take just gets us to the wrong place faster. '
> — Stephen Covey

# 2

# The Magic Elements for Career Fulfilment

*How Does Being Unfulfilled at Work Affect Your Life?*

## The 100,000 Hour Principle

96,750 hours.

What do you think this number represents?

This is the average number of hours a person typically works over their lifetime. Let us do the math:

- 65 (retirement age) – 22 (start of working age) = 43 years
- 43 years x 50 (work weeks a year) x 45 (number of working hours a week) = 96,750 hours

That is nearly 100,000 hours! And if you have chosen to spend your free time reading this book about securing a dream career, something tells me that you will most likely work more than 100,000 hours in your lifetime. I have the same sentiment for the ambitious individuals whom I coach, so I have added 3,250 hours and have called this The 100,000 Hour Principle, as it just sounds more appealing than the 96,750 Hour Principle. The 100,000 Hour Principle is simple: if you are going to work for 100,000 hours, *make choices and take actions that will set you up to enjoy as many of those hours as possible.*

## Are You Working to Live or Living to Work?

A global poll recently conducted by Gallup uncovered that out of the world's roughly one billion full-time workers, only 23 per cent of people are engaged at work. That means that an astronomical 77 per cent of people are unsatisfied in their jobs. These are individuals that Gallup says in its *State of the Global Workplace: 2023 Report* are either 'quiet quitting'—filling a seat, watching the clock and psychologically disconnected from their employer or 'loud quitting' — taking actions that directly harm the organization, undercutting its goals and opposing its leaders.

Whether or not you believe in the idea of career fulfilment and even if you are part of the group that believes in 'working to live', this is a depressing situation.

> 'Where people aren't having fun, they seldom produce good work.' — David Ogilvy

From a macro perspective, Gallup estimates that low engagement costs the global economy $8.8 trillion, accounting for 9 per cent of the global GDP. However, the situation looks even more tragic if you explore the impact that job dissatisfaction has at an individual level.

Not enjoying your job affects much more than those precious 100,000 hours. It can pollute all areas of your life, negatively impacting your mental health, energy levels and relationships. The table below is a representative summary of the answers provided by over 250 working professionals from three different countries when we spoke about how their work life affects other areas of their lives.

| DAILY ROUTINE | MENTAL STATES | |
| --- | --- | --- |
| | Unfulfilled Professionally | Fulfilled Professionally |
| Waking Up | Frustrated, sluggish, dreading the day | Excited, enthusiastic, pulling the day towards them |
| At Work | Bored, managing, surviving, literally counting the hours until they can leave office | Curious, creative, empowered, collaborating with team members |
| After Work | Drained, complaining, numb, closed | Reflecting, sharing, energized or happy-tired |
| Going to Bed | Resigned, annoyed, exhausted | Satisfied, fulfilled, ready for the next day |

We all know what it is like to be around both kinds of people. A person who is fulfilled by their career typically brings more positivity and energy into any space they enter versus a person at the other end of the professional fulfilment spectrum. If someone is spending eight-plus hours of their days in a state of managing or surviving, it takes quite a shift for positivity to flow through them once they leave their place of work.

## 'Colleges Don't Make Fools, They Only Develop Them'

I cannot help but think about this popular quote by the eminent editor, journalist and author George Horace Lorimer as I recall my stint at a reputed business school in India. I was teaching Sports Marketing there. One day, the dean invited me to his office for tea. During our conversation, he proudly shared that his institute had achieved 100 per cent placement for the graduates from the previous year's batch of MBA students. What was not shared but I learnt later was that most of the graduates were placed into one of two large multinational companies and quit within six months, due to complete dissatisfaction with their organization, scope of work and professional environment.

This just left me sad. It meant that after around eighteen years of education, these students were okay with just getting corralled into a job and, possibly, a career pathway they almost certainly would not enjoy. And I know that this situation is not unique to just this one university. This would be the case for most educational institutes around the world that put job placement as a higher priority than career alignment. Given the current placement system, there will be hordes of young professionals across the world right now in careers they do not enjoy. And I am sure, many are dealing with this situation without any clarity or sensible guidance around their next move. This is no way to live.

- Why do we study for so many years only to work in a job or field that does not interest us?
- Why do we remain stuck and frustrated in roles or organizations without making sincere efforts to change our situations?
- Why do we allow outdated systems and people to influence how we spend our 100,000 hours?

It is so natural to head down this path. I was one of those individuals, someone who was ready to allow external forces to dictate the quality of my 100,000 hours. But then I woke up. Not all at once, though. Little by little and step by step, I realized that most of us in the world have an opportunity to skip down a path that will help us enjoy our 100,000 hours and, therefore, live happier lives.

'Good judgment comes from experience, and experience comes from bad judgment.' — Rita Mae Brown

**Three Key Elements to a Successful Career Choice**

- How to have professional fulfilment?
- How do you create a career(s) that leads to inner happiness and fulfilment?
- How do you create a career(s) which is a natural extension of who you are?

It starts with *knowing who you are* and then aligning your career pathway accordingly.

The essence of this approach is focused around three words that you would have most likely heard many times before in multiple contexts:

- passion,
- superpower and
- purpose.

Bear with me here. I am a firm believer that there is no such thing as original thought, there is only original action. What we will be talking about through the rest of the book is how you can reflect on these three words and, through original action, completely transform the experience of your 100,000 hours. I will take you on my journey of self-discovery and introduce you to a formula that has guided every successful career choice I have made over the past twenty years.

We are like organisms in an ecosystem—there are some roles and relationships in which we thrive and others in which we shrink and die. My commitment is to help you create the best possible opportunities to always have careers and professional relationships that allow you to thrive, regardless of the ecosystem, situation or circumstance. Now, let us explore this notion and begin turning it into something that can be practically integrated into your life.

Help me, help *you*.

'Everyone has been made for some particular work and the desire for that work has been put in every heart.' — Rumi

# 3

# Pursue Your Passion

*What Are You Deeply Interested in?*

## My Happy Place

Grinning like a Cheshire cat, Jim said, 'Neel, today is the big day. Today is the day that we are going to figure out your future career.'

The year was 1995, and I was in the posh office of my private career counsellor, Jim, in Laguna Beach, California. Like many desi parents, my folks wanted to get ahead of the game when it came to figuring out my career and, ultimately, my life's plan. They felt that the ripe old age of fifteen years was just the right time to start this process. So, there I was sitting in front of Jim's large, wooden desk, feeling both nervous and excited as this gentle giant smiled at me. He was holding the results of the comprehensive career aptitude test he had me take the previous week.

As he handed me three file folders, I enthusiastically grabbed them from his hands and looked at the first one, which was labelled 'banking'. It was full of a stack of papers with information about how to get into banking, types of companies to work with, the salary range, what universities the best bankers graduated from, etc.

I quickly glanced at the contents and then put the folder aside and less enthusiastically picked up the second one. This one was labelled 'business analyst'. I was dumbfounded at this point because I did not even know that this was a job, and, at the time, I was not very fond of business or analysis, so it seemed odd that I would be primed for a career which combines both. I did not even bother to look in the folder, as I knew that the information contained inside would not interest me at all. Instead, I started becoming aware that my stomach was beginning to knot and some sweat beads were forming on my head. It is nearly the same feeling as watching my favourite team, Liverpool FC, playing a match I felt they should easily win but then was up with one penalty shot left, where a miss would mean getting knocked out of an important cup competition.

But my situation required some serious praying as this could impact the rest of my life. I reluctantly peeked in the third folder, hoping that it would say something of interest to me. The word 'accountant' showed up, and I threw the folders back onto Jim's table with more force than appropriate, wondering if his stupid career test suggestion machine was broken. Mom quickly picked up the folders and said with full affection and slight desperation to ensure something good came out of the $1,500 she spent on Jim's counselling sessions, 'Son, which one of these options do you want to choose?'

I did not answer because I was no longer there. Well, physically I was, but mentally I had checked out. I retreated to a time just a few weeks earlier when I was in Denmark participating in an international football tournament called the Dana Cup. (Although I am a California kid who grew up calling the sport soccer, I intentionally refer to the beautiful game as football throughout the book for consistency.)

I was not just remembering the goals that I scored and the matches my club team Orange Coast United won. I was deeply engrossed in reminiscing about the conversations that I had with teenagers from all over the world. And how I felt at one with myself, my teammates and the other footballers while we watched a top-flight European match on a small black-and-white television. The pure joy I experienced over the week being around the sport I loved. I was jolted out of this beautiful memory with the sound of Jim's deep and slightly irritated voice saying, 'Neel, which career option do you want to work towards moving forward?'

And suddenly from a place beyond my conscious mind, I replied, 'Jim, I don't want to be a banker, business analyst or accountant, I only want to work in football.'

Suddenly, the tension in the room dissipated as Mom and Jim burst out laughing. In response, I simply closed my eyes and travelled back to my happy place at the football tournament in Denmark.

The fifteen-year-old me sitting in Jim's office was crystal clear about what my passion was: football. I started playing the sport when I was four years old and immediately fell in love. A typical day for me when I was fifteen would look something like this: Wake up and read all the high school and university football scores in the *LA Times* during breakfast. Go to school and play football during class breaks with friends. Train with my high school team after classes. Get home and play a few games of *FIFA* on PlayStation. Go to my travel team training, come home, shower and play a few more games of *FIFA*. Wind down the day by quickly eating dinner and then watching VHS cassette tapes of the 1994 FIFA World Cup until it was time to go to bed, often discussing my favourite football moments with my brother, Paras, until I finally fell asleep.

Clearly, my passion was football. Even today, over two decades later, while my passions have evolved (it is perfectly normal for them to change or evolve), I am still deeply connected to the sport. And I want to be clear—there is nothing wrong with working as a banker, a business analyst, or an accountant. Some of my best friends have fulfilling and lucrative careers in these fields. It is just that my teenage self was sure that these positions were not in line with who I was. I might have been unsure about what I wanted to do in my life, but I certainly liked the idea of making my passion my pay cheque.

Or as Bob Dylan put it, 'What's money? A man is a success if he gets up in the morning and goes to bed at night and in between does what he wants to do.'

What is *your* passion?

You do not know?

Struggling?

You are not alone. People struggle with identifying the areas of life that deeply interest them. It is quite funny that although we live with ourselves twenty-four hours a day, there is so much that we still do not know or understand about who we are.

## How to Find Your Passion

You can begin by answering the following questions:

- What would I do for free?
- What activities make me feel truly alive or give me a sense of pure joy?

- What activities make me lose track of time?
- What topics do I love to discuss and ponder?
- What in life gives me an irresistible sense of inspiration, a reason to get out of bed?

## Do *Not* Channel Your Inner Couch Potato

If you reflect upon these with sincerity, each of these questions can open up a window into you, revealing so much. Take, for example, the last question about what gives you a reason to get out of bed. Paras was always a self-diagnosed 'procrastinator'. On weekends, he would wake up after noon, sleepwalk to the couch and watch sports for the rest of the day, typically until it was time to go to bed. This lethargic attitude trickled into his professional life as well. Predictably, it led to multiple terminations that impacted the quality of his life financially, mentally and emotionally. And it could have severely impacted his marriage as on the day of his wedding, he forgot to bring an important document, which delayed the start of the ceremony by nearly an hour, leaving the guests wondering if it was the bride or the groom who took off running.

Paras's inability to focus and follow discipline was a major issue in our family because Dad was a self-made man. He grew up in a farming village in Gujarat, as the eldest son in a family of eight children. Through his intelligence, hard work and determination, he moved to the United States and created opportunities for his siblings to shift base to the West and settle down. Given Dad's success, it was assumed by everyone in our family and community that Paras would carry the torch forward, achieve professional success and 'make lots of money'. There was a tremendous amount of expectation and pressure put on him to succeed and make everyone proud. Paras instead dropped out of the University of California and essentially gave up on pursuing formal education.

How did my family react?

How do you *think* they would react?

Something like this can greatly impact a family. And it did. My parents were deeply shocked and disappointed. There were constant arguments in our home accompanied with long, heated debates about whether or not someone needs a degree to succeed and what Paras was now going to do with his life. I hated those times and really prayed hard that Paras would re-enrol into his university and complete his degree. As the entitled younger brother, I had no problem telling him this every time we spoke. I was not concerned about what he wanted to do. All I cared about was that he does what everyone else wants him to do so that we can go back to having a happy home, and the uncles and aunties would not judge him or my parents.

Instead, I watched him suffer through his twenties and early thirties, never really finding his professional path, nor getting over the disappointment he caused my family by dropping out of university after just one year. He was always on survival mode, taking jobs that paid the bills instead of going for what he really wanted to do. He was approaching the job market as a 'college dropout' instead of someone who had gifts to contribute to the world. And what good company wants to hire a professionally insecure individual?

It was only after I discovered my unique formula for creating a dream career and validated its effectiveness by working with a few others that I started to work with Paras. Because my friend, 'there's a difference between knowing the path and walking the path'. Trust the wise Morpheus to put things in perspective.

*Did Paras really ask himself what he wanted to do?*

No!

So, I decided to slice up the couch potato and deep fry it.

We began by spending some time identifying his passion. He thought his passion was sports, given that he spent most of his waking hours watching sports or talking about sports. However, when I asked him about his 'reason to get out of bed or couch in his case', it sparked something inside of him. After some serious soul-searching, he realized that while consuming sports is something that he likes, his true passion was connected to live events.

*Bingo*!

He shared that he did not like to wake up so late but did so because he did not *feel* like he had any pressing reason to get up in the morning. I asked him what would get him excited to wake up early, and he shared 'events, any type of event, sports, music, networking, anything where people get together for something fun or interesting'. Then he proudly walked me through what he did in the hours before heading out for the charity golf tournament he had recently planned. An exercise intended to prove that he loved events and had it within himself to be productive:

- Day before the golf tournament
    □ Went to the supply store and purchased all remaining items required for event
    □ Messaged volunteers the final instructions and confirmed pick-up time
    □ Loaded the car with remaining supplies
    □ Messaged everyone to get their coffee order
    □ Slept by 9:30 p.m.
- Day of the golf tournament
    □ Woke up by 4:30 a.m.

- Gave each volunteer a wake-up call
- Went to the local coffee shop and purchased coffee for volunteers
- Picked up each volunteer and headed to the golf course

This was *my* brother!

I was amazed that this person who struggled to wake up before noon on most weekends and arrived late for work on many weekdays, could so comfortably transform into a highly responsible and organized programme director or events planner when it involved designing and delivering an event or experience. The thrill of being part of a live event drove him to break the old pattern of lethargy.

The more we journeyed into his past, the more it became clear that Paras was always happiest before, during and even after any sort of an event. Be it my youth football matches that he religiously attended every weekend for over ten years, or all of the professional sporting events we would go to or the annual music festivals he could not miss. Even today, Paras and my sister-in-law, Jeanne, both in their forties, childless, and, yet, are proud holders of annual passes for Disneyland, Universal Studios, Magic Mountain and Knott's Berry Farm. And, trust me, these are not like the gym memberships that you excitedly purchase on 1 January, use for a week and then forget. These passes are worn out due to the number of times they have been swiped through the ticket machines at the entrance gates of these popular amusement parks.

Although Paras enjoyed the self-reflection process and reminiscing about all the events he had attended in the past, he kept saying, 'Everyone likes live events, how could this be my passion?'

So we went through the self-reflection questions again and wrote out his answers on a whiteboard. What emerged was clear as day: 'live events' was something that Paras was genuinely passionate about. Nothing else gives him the thrill that he gets when being around large crowds and an endless assortment of fun activities. Finally, Paras accepted this to be his truth.

So, ask yourself the right questions because this can unlock opportunities you did not even realize existed and take your career (and life) to new heights. Every such question will open up a new pathway, which may not always lead to success, but when you find the right question to ask it can be the key to unlocking something extraordinary.

Because 'Under this pressure, under this weight, we are all diamonds taking shape ...'

## Identify Your Red Flags

Avantika, my wife, had a completely different life experience from that of Paras. She grew up in New Delhi as the daughter of two successful doctors. As an intelligent, hard-working student, she sucessfully secured her master's degree in psychology from the University of Delhi. The combination of a prominent university and good grades made the placement process seamless for her. And a few months before she graduated, she received an attractive offer from a well-known Fortune 500 consulting firm.

After nearly nineteen years of education, the 'light at the end of the tunnel' finally emerged with a position with a high-profile company. It had all the elements that any young professional looks for: an office located in a hi-fi commercial district, guaranteed business travel and the opportunity to consult some of the biggest companies in the world. This achievement was complemented by the encouragement from her family who did not know much about the field but were reassured with the fact that they had heard of the company. With the momentum heading in one direction, Avantika chose not to interview with any other company and proudly accepted the offer to join this organization as a 'talent and leadership consultant'.

Anyone who could see her world from the outside would say that her professional life was set. Within her first year at the company, she was given the opportunity to travel and work with some of the company's marquee clients, awarded for her achievements and was due for a promotion. And while she was grateful for all of this, she was not truly happy. She was not feeling fulfilled and did not see that changing, no matter what adjustments were made to her role. This was a red flag and led her to look within.

Because sometimes, as the great poet Robert Lowell once said, 'The light at the end of the tunnel is just the light of an oncoming train.'

When Avantika started this exercise, it did not take long for her to realize that her passion was the arts. As a child, she was always happiest while painting, making cards, picking flowers, singing, dancing, playing and creating games, new words and new languages. As a teenager, she would spend hours getting lost in creativity through writing, art and reflecting on ideas, poetry and music. Engaging with the arts is what she would happily do for free, what would make her feel alive, make her lose track of time. It is what she loves to learn about, discuss and ponder. The arts are a source of inspiration for her. It was clear that her position at the consulting firm did not include any connection to the arts, and there was a limited possibility that it would at any given point in the future.

However, Avantika did not leave the Fortune 500 company and become an artist. Nor did Paras immediately quit his job and become an event planner. This is part of a process. Self-reflection gave Paras and Avantika an insight into themselves and what truly made them happy and gave them a sense of pure joy.

Remember my Wild Rivers experience? I thought what I really liked was sitting around in the sun at the water park, but then I quickly realized that this was not my passion. That this was just something I enjoyed doing in the summer with friends.

What happens when we have multiple passions? In Paras's case and in the case of many others who have undergone this exercise, I have found that when you authentically answer the self-reflection questions, one passion comes to the surface, which takes precedent over the others. That said, it is perfectly acceptable to do this work using multiple passions, something which I have addressed later in the book.

Look within yourself to see what truly makes you happy and makes you feel alive. It is not always the first thing that comes to mind, as your head is not always the best evaluator of your true self. This answer usually comes from the heart (emotional intelligence) or the body (somatic intelligence), places that you can access easier as you silence the monkey mind.

'I am burdened with what the Buddhists call the "monkey mind"— the thoughts that swing from limb to limb, stopping only to scratch themselves, spit and howl.'— Elizabeth Gilbert

Do not be. Remember, the journey to discover your passion or passions is most often experiential and not just cognitive or derived through thought. So as you engage with the world, let your heart and body give you clues on whether or not you are on the right path until you feel that you have identified your true passion. This is one of the first steps in the process of creating *your dream career*.

> 'Find out what you like doing best and get someone to pay you for doing it.' — Katharine Whitehorn

# 4

# Tap into Your Superpower

*What Are You Extraordinary at?*

'Heroes are made by the path they choose, not the powers
they are graced with.' — *Iron Man*

## And the Hero Lies in You ...

Like most kids, growing up, I was fascinated by superheroes,
all superheroes, fictional or real-life. Paras and I filled our
weekends by enjoying the feats of our superheroes. We found
the same excitement and awe watching Batman defeat the
Joker for the hundredth time with his strength and intelligence
as we did while watching Diego Maradona gracefully dribble
past the entire English national team defence to score a goal.
The common thread was that each one was doing something
extraordinary, leaving others in a state of delight.

Why did we love superheroes? Because they represent
hope, opportunity and strength for everybody.

Could I be a superhero? No way!

What went into becoming one?

I had no clue!

I was just enthralled watching these fictional characters and real-life athletes do what they do best. However, over time, I realized that becoming a superhero is just about unlocking your superpowers (*yes, we all have them*) and using them.

Each of us is born with a mind, body and spirit; however, most of us differ in what provides nourishment for these core elements of our being.

What nourishes you?

Eating a hearty meal, getting a massage, listening to soulful music or spending time with close friends?

These activities bring forth the 'feel-good' factor, but they do not nourish your mind, body and spirit on a sustained basis.

From what I have come to understand, God/Universal Power/Nature/whatever you want to call the force that drives the universe has provided us with unique sets of talents that, when manifested in the world, give us a sense of fulfilment. These talents are our very own superpowers, which offer inner nourishment when used effectively.

Yes, you heard that right. *You have a superpower.*

More importantly, when we utilize these talents, we can contribute to the world in an authentic and impactful way. I call this living an extraordinarily natural life.

These days, in a world where society places tremendous value on power, profile and material wealth, many people choose the road most travelled. Often, this means letting go of their special talents at an early age in order to pursue a job in a field for reasons that may not serve them in the long run.

'You either die a hero or live long enough to see yourself become the villain.'— *Dark Knight*

Make a choice. Make it *now*!

Imagine if Wolverine chose not to use his claws to fight his enemies. It sounds silly; however, this is what happens in the world on a minute-by-minute basis. People choose to disregard their superpowers to follow a path that is not truly theirs. Those who choose to unlock their superpowers and create a life where they can regularly use these innate talents become extraordinary. However, to me, it is the most natural way to live.

## What Is a Superpower?

A superpower is a special or unique power or ability that you are born with. These are not just reserved for fictional characters; every human has a superpower. Superpowers are not restricted to world-saving abilities like being able to see the future, read people's minds or become invisible. *Superpowers can be ordinary strengths*. And by identifying your superpower, you can get closer to choosing a career where you would most likely experience high performance and growth as well as joy and contentment.

## What Are Not Superpowers?

Superpowers are strengths, not skills. A skill is something that you can learn and master through repetition, while a strength is something that you are naturally good at and need not necessarily have to learn. For example, your skill is knowing how to speak Spanish, but your ability to learn languages quickly is your strength. Being able to design an effective life coaching plan is a skill; however, tapping into your natural ability to be a compassionate, curious listener is a strength. You may forget a skill you learnt, but your strength(s) lasts a lifetime.

## How to Find Your Superpower

Ask yourself the following questions:

- What are my strengths?
- What abilities come naturally to me?
- Where do I see the most results in my life? Why?
- What do the people I trust most say that I excel at?
- What activities give me energy?
- During what activities am I in the 'flow' or totally absorbed and immersed in my work?

This will take some work and time. Sometimes your superpower will be so obvious and natural that you would not even think that it is a superpower. The reality around superpowers is that we arrive in this world with these natural talents. Then we spend part of our lives, abandoning them or letting others diminish their importance. Because of this, we quickly lose connection with our true self and allow others who do not have a sense of who we are, pressure us into fitting into various societal roles. Thus, completely neglecting and negating the power of our unique and innate strengths.

'There is a superhero in all of us. We just need the courage to put on the cape.' — *Superman*

## How Did I Discover My Superpower?

Well, it came to me when I went through certain situations in my life where I saw extremely positive outcomes at times when I was just being my natural self. Let me share a couple of these.

My tenth birthday was quickly approaching, and my parents were planning to organize a small party for me to celebrate my first decade on this earth. They decided to have the party at a venue outside of our home and let me choose the place. I spent the next few days thinking about every possible option and then saw an ad in our local newspaper about a new roller-skating rink that has opened in our hometown of Fountain Valley. Shortly afterwards, we ended up taking a short drive down to Fountain Valley Skating Center to check if it would fit my long list of requirements.

The place was shiny and new, and full of everything that a ten-year-old could ever dream of for his birthday party. It had massive roller-skating rink, organized competitions, an endless selection of video games and every option of junk food you can imagine. When we told the lovely girl at the reception that we were thinking of hosting my tenth birthday party at their new establishment, they immediately rolled out the red carpet for us. Paras and I got a free tutorial on how to skate backwards with speed and control from their hotshot skating coach, played every video game we wanted to and nourished ourselves with hot, cheesy slices of pepperoni pizza, washing it all down with ice-cold cherry coke. To top it all off, the staff showed us the new hi-fi laser strobe lights they had recently installed and gave us parting gifts of two pairs of cool skating wrist guards and key chains that had roller skates dangling from the ring.

I was over the moon when I left the skating centre. There could have been no better place in the world to host my party. Although my birthday was still a month away, as soon as we got home, I pestered Mom into booking the party package immediately, which she did, and all was well in life. I invited twenty-five of my best friends to the party but then could not help but tell everyone in my outer circle that 'Neel Shah's tenth birthday roller-skating experience' will be simply amazing. That people will not be the same after they try out the one-of-a-kind roller-skating lesson, participate in the fun competitions, eat the best pizza ever and play the biggest collection of arcade games in Fountain Valley!

Having a big mouth has bigger repercussions which I clearly had no clue about.

As I went to town about my forthcoming grand party, Mom was drowned with requests from parents for their kids to be invited to my birthday party. The next thing we know is that my party, which was planned for a humble group of twenty-five people, turned into the party of the year with seventy-five of my classmates present. I had barely spoken with these kids who showed up at the centre, birthday present in hand, and sporting their best roller-skating outfit. I obviously got an earful from my folks because my avatar of a broadcaster significantly impacted their budget, though they were impressed with my ability to entice nearly half of my fifth-grade class to navigate their way onto my invite list. But then 'you don't choose your avatar, your avatar chooses you'.

Fast forward thirteen years. It was 2003, and I was living in Brooklyn in a neighbourhood called Park Slope. I loved living in New York in my twenties and was crazy about Park Slope. I ensured that I weaved this into every phone conversation with three of my best friends from college, Phil, Courtney and Stephanie, who, at the time, were living and working in California. After a year of this narrative, they ended up moving to The Big Apple. And not just to any borough, they moved to Brooklyn, and not just any part of Brooklyn, they all moved to within a one-mile radius from me in Park Slope.

Magic?

'Magic is just science that we don't understand yet.'
— Arthur C. Clarke

And the science at play here was that I was using my superpower. See, while I was good at playing football, it was not my superpower as there were many people much better than me, so there was no way that I could consider playing this sport as my extraordinary ability. My superpower was something that had nothing to do with sport. It was the reason behind why seventy-five kids turned up for my tenth birthday party and why three of my best friends left their jobs and moved across the country into the same neighbourhood where I was living. Heck, it is the reason why I am writing this book.

What is my superpower?

*I can get people interested in or excited about something that has touched, moved or inspired me.*

As I said, it need not be of the Batman and Superman kind; it is *extraordinarily ordinary.* I am wired to be someone who will share, share, share and share some more about whatever it is that has impacted my life in a way that moves something within the listener. It could be a book or a movie recommendation, which people immediately integrate into their plans. Or possibly a spiritual practice that I follow, which becomes the daily routine of those who hear about it from me. I am wired with a deep and profound enthusiasm about wanting others to experience what makes me happy and with the right set of vocal cords, vocabulary, vulnerability and energy to be effective when I do so.

How do I know that?

I could figure this all out by picking up clues from my life experience and answering the self-reflection questions, which had me honestly look at my life and the places where I see the most results. Being average in most areas, it is hard to pinpoint where I stand out in anything. However, when I reflected on my life and spoke with those I trust, it became abundantly clear that I have a unique ability to impact people when I honestly share about products, people, places, concepts, or experiences that have had a positive impact on me.

The beautiful thing about your superpower is that when you share this gift with others, when it comes from a place that is natural to you, it will renew them and you in the process. On the other hand, when you give something away that is unnatural or forced, it leaves you feeling low and depleted of energy. I can be with one person or millions of people speaking about something which has positively impacted me for hours without ever tiring. This experience constantly renews my energy and gives me a high. It is an incomparable feeling. This is not the case when I am engaged for hours in an activity that is forced upon me, which unfortunately is the reality for many people when it comes to the scope of their professional responsibilities.

## Live Your Dreams, Not Your Fears

We had determined earlier that Paras's passion was live events. However, many years of professional disappointments had led him to regularly question his strengths. I have found that it is harder for older people to gain clarity and confidence around their superpower. Why?

This is primarily because they carry so much baggage from past challenges that their minds will not let them believe that they have a superpower.

Remember the iconic dialogue from the movie *Batman Begins*? 'You always fear what you don't understand.' Reflect on that because as Oprah Winfrey once said, 'Courage is feeling the fear and doing it anyway.'

I am glad my brother chose to live a better life. As I took Paras through the self-reflection questions something interesting began to emerge. He identified that the people he trusted most always counted on him to organize activities for them, and that his events were always top-notch. This became even more apparent as we got to the fifth question as he shared that organizing events always gave him energy. It was during the planning and execution stages of an event when Paras was working as his best self or in the flow. After multiple introspective sittings, he found his core strength.

What is Paras's superpower?

*He is exceptionally strong at organizing engaging experiences for people.*

Since we were kids, he would use his high IQ and limitless energy to make up games on the spot using bar stools, laundry baskets, flower pots, whatever was around. He would ensure that our friends and family were never bored, as his activities could last for hours. As he grew older, this turned into organizing concerts and festivals at his university, and then curating unique events for Long Beach residents like 'Shop with a Cop' or 'Speed Dating with a Twist'. However, until we started our sessions, Paras had always seen event management as something he did on the side for fun, not as a career.

'A man is but a product of his thoughts. What he thinks he becomes.' — Mahatma Gandhi

Avantika on the other hand, initially found it difficult to identify her superpower, as she is one of the most humble people one could ever meet. She would be the last person at a dinner table to share something about herself because she would not want to take the limelight away from anyone else. This humility is one of her most endearing qualities hence she refused to acknowledge that there was something that she was better at compared to most people. We went through each of the self-reflection questions over multiple sittings, barely filling up my whiteboard with anything of note.

Understandably, she became frustrated with me and the process, feeling that I was trying to force her into having a superpower when she did not have one.

*'Nobody said it was easy*
*No one ever said it would be so hard ...'*

It was during this time, though, that something became crystal clear to me. No matter how frustrated or angry she got, it is so challenging to be anything but calm in her presence.

This was something that I had known since we first met at the Nataraj Dance Festival hosted at Zorba the Buddha in New Delhi. During the week of getting to know one another at the festival, I found her presence to be delightful, and she seemed at peace with herself and those around her. She would ask questions and use her ears and *heart* to listen to the answers, and she never felt the need to impose her ego into any conversation. She was a joy to be around because she would make everyone who interacted with her feel heard and accepted. I assumed that this was 'festival Avantika' and that she would be a completely different person once we returned home. But as we started dating, I realized her presence was just as pleasant in the middle of New Delhi traffic on a Friday evening, as it was in the gorgeous environs of Zorba the Buddha.

Our families and friends validated that her presence is calming to be around. Just to be sure, we went through the self-reflection questions multiple times. While answers like 'creativity' or 'being caring' came up when we wrote her responses onto the whiteboard, nothing felt as accurate to her as the original one suggested by me and endorsed by our near and dear ones.

What is Avantika's superpower?

*She can make people feel at ease in her presence.*

Interacting with her will calm you. This is not something that she studied or even practised; it is how she is wired and how she naturally engages with the world. This is a perfect example of a superpower that is so natural to one's own being that it is difficult to accept that this is, in fact, a superpower.

That is the thing with identifying your own superpower— it is not always the obvious answer, and, often, it is a part of yourself that you may have never given much thought to.

I was well into my career when I realized that my superpower was getting people interested in or excited about something that has touched, moved or inspired me. For Paras and Avantika, it took multiple sessions, extensive self-reflection, and committed loved ones to identify and fully accept their superpowers. It is not always going with the low-hanging fruit answer. Take the time to explore various options and see what feels right to you and to those whom you trust.

## Your Next Step

Spend some time exploring your superpower. Do not just explore this from a career perspective, but from what people say you excel at, where you see the most results in your life, or what activities help you get in the flow, or give you energy.

*And you will definitely be able to tap into your superpower.* Once you have some clarity around your superpower, write it down and examine how it shows up in your life.

Unlocked multiple superpowers? Good. Reflect on them, and we will address how to work with this phenomenon later in the book.

Now that you have found your passion and superpower finding your purpose will be a cakewalk. *Yes*, it will be. Do not look at life as a puzzle waiting to be solved—live it, love it, experience it.

'Your talent is God's gift to you. What you do with it is your gift back to God.' — Leo Buscaglia

# 5

# Live Your Purpose in Life

*How Do You Want to Contribute to the World?*

## My Journey from Zero to Hero

'I don't want him, look at his complexion, he looks and smells like poo.'

I wish the captain of the football team meant Winnie-the-Pooh!

It was 1984.

I was four years old and standing in the middle of a football pitch with my kindergarten classmates. I was praying that one of the captains of the recess football teams would pick me soon, so I could show off my skills that I developed after a summer of practising with Paras in our backyard. But everyone got picked except me.

My head dropped, and I did everything possible to hold back my tears and disappear into the grass. This type of experience can be hard to process for any child, especially when you are one of the few South Asians living in a primarily white neighbourhood in a predominantly white Southern Californian suburban city. Thankfully, the other captain traded one of his players to the other team and took me on his, or I may have just given up football forever.

The match started, and my sadness disappeared immediately after I scored my first goal. The hole in my heart created by my naive classmate was soon filled with joy and a sense of belonging when my teammates jumped all over me and screamed my name after I scored my fifth goal. I went from feeling like a zero to becoming the schoolyard hero in the matter of one recreational football match. So what if I looked different from the rest of the people around me?

## Finding My Purpose in Life

'What are the two most important days in your life? The day you are born and the day you find out why.'— Mark Twain

This love for football continued throughout my childhood. It was football that allowed me to feel at home in my skin, social circle and country. It was football that provided my parents with the opportunity to build a community of American friends. It was football that created a pathway for me to travel outside of the United States for the first time and it was football that gave me a reason to wake up each day. So, when I looked at my purpose and explored how I wanted to contribute to the world, it was no surprise that my answer was *to create opportunities for people to grow through football*, as this sport had given me so much both on and off the pitch.

Why is it important for you to know your purpose when you are exploring your dream job?

If you approach your professional life as an opportunity to serve versus an opportunity to receive, you will have a more fulfilling career. It is inevitable that even when you have your dream job or are working for a dream company, things will not always go well. Your boss will anger you. Your client will push you too far. You will have a challenging member of your team. Your customers will annoy you. You will not get the promotion that you feel you deserve. It is especially during these times that it is essential to see your work as a platform to serve humanity in a way that aligns with what is important to you.

This is not advice; this comes from direct experience. Whenever my colleagues or I saw our job as a 'means to an end', we would be bogged down by the day-to-day challenges, which come up in any profession. We were just dealing with the daily grind as it comes. However, when we saw our professional responsibilities as an opportunity to contribute to the world, our entire experience of our work and working environment would get transformed.

'Your purpose in life is to find your purpose and give your whole heart and soul to it.' — Gautam Buddha

## How Would You Like to Contribute to the World?

The following self-reflection questions should help you answer the above:

- What is an area of life where I am already contributing and making an impact?
- What do I want the world to have more of?
- What is an area of life that I would like to transform?

- What is something that has significantly impacted my life that I would like to pay forward?
- What is an issue affecting my family, community, state, country, planet, etc., that I want to address?

While discovering your purpose, it is key to focus on the *why* and *who* instead of getting too wrapped up in the *how* and *what*. And, like your superpower, know that your purpose comes from your inner self and is rarely something that you actively choose. It is by looking within that you are able to identify your core values and beliefs that you hold most dear and make them a guiding force in your life. An inner compass. You can never truly understand how to find your purpose by listening to others' opinions, seeking outside approval or running from one commitment to another. That said, do pay attention to what service communities you resonate with as this can offer you some clues about your purpose.

During the career creation work with Paras, we looked at several different ways in which he wanted to contribute to the world, until we honed in on what he was already doing and who he had already been. Paras has room for the whole world to fit in his heart. If you meet him, he will hug you and acknowledge you for something. He goes out of his way to make others happy through banter, jokes, service or organizing fun events. Even during his darkest days, he would find a way to make those around him feel at home. You could say that he is a complete 'people's person'.

As we went through the self-reflection questions in detail, what emerged was that his purpose in life *was making people happy,* which is something that he strives for through every interaction he has. He lives to bring happiness to others, and it hurts him when he is unable to do this. Paras confirmed that this was indeed his purpose.

Avantika did not take long to identify and accept her purpose in life. She has always been empathetic to people's feelings through her capacity to make space for all emotions, especially difficult ones like sadness, pain, loneliness, confusion, feeling misunderstood or marginalized. She explored ways in which she could help others through active listening, expressive arts engagement or non-judgemental and compassionate dialogue to bring people more in connection to themselves and others. Also, practising Buddhism for many years greatly helped as it allowed her to regularly connect with the highest potential in herself and others. These experiences always left her feeling enlivened and empowered.

At the consulting firm, in her 'dream job', her specific role was focused on researching and creating products for its clients to improve organizational efficiency. She was great at her job, but she soon realized that something was missing ...

When we met the following year, we went through the self-reflection questions and revisited her personal and professional situations to identify her energy levels, focus areas and emotions. What emerged was Avantika saw that her purpose was *to create spaces for people to heal and feel empowered*. Based on her practical experiences while studying psychology, she knew she loved working with individuals and small groups and directly impacting their growth. Since this was an area of life where she was already contributing and making an impact, she wanted the world to have more of it. We then came up with imaginary scenarios to explore how it would feel to integrate this purpose fully into her professional life. She felt joyful about the idea of creating a full-time career where facilitating human growth would be the primary focus. Imagining yourself in various professional scenarios is an important step in the process of identifying your dream career. It allows your mind and body to get a sense of what it could look and feel like to experience a particular professional environment and scope of work. This exercise can lead to insights and clues about what resonates and what does not.

Approaching your career as a way to serve does not mean that you must live your life like Mahatma Gandhi or Mother Teresa! So, you can breathe easy now.

Just look to build purpose in your professional activities. Never take your eyes off the bigger picture, even during the most demanding or frustrating work challenges. It gives you access to that additional energy source within yourself so that you can manage, expand and grow in your role and organization on a day-to-day basis. It ensures that you treat your colleagues, customers, clients, vendors and everyone else connected to your work as teammates, not competitors.

'Having a purpose is the difference between making a living and making a life.' — Tom Thiss

When your work is aligned with how you want to contribute to the world, you somehow become lighter as you know that you are living your purpose. The world needs something, and you are there to provide it through your professional commitments. And there is a lot the world needs, so there will be endless ways to contribute to this giant planet that matches how you want to serve.

Go through the self-reflection questions and take steps to identify your purpose. Try not to get caught up in financial projections and logistics; just be with the questions and let the answers emerge from your core being. Keep your eyes open, look for reoccurring patterns and, most importantly, listen to your body whenever it signals to you that something is meaningful. Trust that your body knows exactly what really matters to you and sensations are its way of communicating. Your body serves as the best source of truth and intuition before they are impacted by any limiting beliefs stored in your mind.

'Life is never made unbearable by circumstances, but only by lack of meaning and purpose.' — Viktor Frankl

# 6

# Perfect Your Mission Statement

*How Do You Make Your Words Your World?*

## My Mission Statement: Weapon or Armour?

When I look back, the episode at Jim's office was a godsend. Although Mom thought she had wasted thousands of dollars on career counselling sessions that I did not take seriously, I saw things differently. It took these sessions and the file folders full of information on careers that I did not want to look deep within myself and realize that I aspired to work in the football industry.

By writing off the other 'aligned' career choices, listening to my intuition, no matter how silly it may have sounded at the time and declaring what I wanted, something happened: I had planted a seed. And, as we all know, planting a seed in soil is the beginning of the creation of a new organism that has the power to nurture and give life to generations of others. Now it was time to nurture that seed so that it manifests into a career pathway that is aligned with how I would want to serve the world.

I cannot stress how important it is to have a sense of what you do *not* want to gain clarity on what you do. Otherwise, you will be pulled in multiple directions through external pressures or fly by night trends. While I understood that each of those presented career options could lead to positions that offered power, prestige and financial security, I just knew that they were not for me. I was a quick learner, organized and disciplined, and confident that I would be able to hack it as a banker, business analyst or accountant if I worked hard enough. However, I was clear that these careers were not in line with who I was and how I would like to serve the world professionally.

On a lighter note:

'Follow your passion. Stay true to yourself. Never follow anyone else's path unless you're in the woods and you're lost and you see a path. Then, by all means, follow that path.'
— Ellen DeGeneres

But you know what I mean …

Great! One problem solved. The following question may arise in your mind in the teething stage: How do I take what I feel aligned with and how I want to serve the world professionally, and make it a reality?

Just knowing that I want a career in the professional football industry would not be enough to lead to anything tangible, nor would it inspire confidence in those around me.

Then what was I left with?

Well, other than highly concerned and slightly frustrated parents, I was left with a starting point. At least I knew my passion. Over the next few days, I started watering the seed that I planted through research, conversations with anyone connected to professional football and visualization exercises where I would picture myself working in the industry.

It was important not to appear as a headless chicken. Or sound like a broken record pretty much saying the same thing and doing nothing.

'What makes you think the football industry will want to hire you over the hundreds of millions of people who also like this sport?'

'What value are you going to add to the football industry?'

'What do you want to do in football?'

'If you are not going to be a professional player, will you become the coach?'

These were a few questions thrown my way.

I wish I had the answers ...

Was I embarrassed?

Hell, yes!

But thanks to these questions by some of my exasperated friends and family, I made a decision.

I found a quiet place, took out my notebook and wrote down all the reasons why I wanted to work in football and why I felt I would do a great job in the industry. Did I know anything about the business of the sport?

Obviously not!

So, I just focused on why I loved the game and how that love could contribute to the development of footballers and the sport as a whole.

Finally, a mission statement began to emerge about my dream job, which I could comfortably share with the world.

Ever played a video game?

Doing this exercise made me feel as if I was unlocking a new weapon, which made it easier for me to get from one zone to another.

'If passion drives you, let reason hold the reins.'
— Benjamin Franklin

A mission statement is extremely important in the life of a confused teenager, especially a desi one. *Why?* It greatly helps in making it through any dinner table, wedding, or cultural event conversation about 'what I want to do when I grow up'. It helped me immensely. Because I had the *wonderful opportunity* to share my plans with someone every week. Sometimes I felt that my family, friends and well-wishers were just testing me to see if I may change my answer if caught off guard. But I stayed true to my commitment to working in football ...

Unfortunately, in 1995 the football industry was not established in the United States. Although the 1994 FIFA World Cup was a massive success averaging over 69,000 spectators a match, by 1995 it was a distant memory. The original North American Soccer League (NASL) folded in 1984, and other than the Continental Indoor Soccer League, a fledgling indoor football competition that eventually folded in 1997, and college football, there was not much happening in the professional football scene. Most of the positions in youth football at the time were either for volunteers or for individuals interested in working as coaches, sporting directors, fitness trainers or administrators which was neither my interest nor strength.

## The Power of Manifestation

Regardless, I kept at it, speaking to anyone who cared to listen. Then something incredible happened, which initiated my belief in the power of intention—a belief that has only deepened over the decades.

It was April 1995; I woke up and went through my typical morning ritual of showering, getting dressed and devouring a bowl of my favourite cereal (Cinnamon Toast Crunch if you really want to know), while I read the *LA Times* before rushing out of the door to high school. I was about to put the main paper aside to find the sports pages, when something on its front page caught my eye. The word 'soccer' was written in big, bold letters, which in 1995 was unexpected. I looked closer at the page, and to my surprise and excitement, it was a story about how a professional football league called Major League Soccer (MLS) would be launched in 1996 with ten teams spread across the country. My heart expanded, and I felt butterflies in my stomach as I knew that my prayers had been answered.

'The power of manifestation is being able to harness your true destinies and desires in life, subconsciously putting them into a vision and then into reality. It is knowing that everything you want of the universe is already yours, and the clearer your thoughts and thinking are on the matter, the more timely and precise the delivery will come.'

Mindset coach Elise Micheals shared her views on the immense power of manifestation with me during a recent conversation.

Rhonda Byrne made this a mainstream concept in her best-selling book *The Secret* in 2006, a good ten years after my own experience of this incredible law of the universe.

Finally, I could connect my professional aspirations to a tangible organization. I had something to work towards as I built my professional competency! And I had ammunition that would quieten my inner circle of 'pessimist well-wishers'. But then 'a lion doesn't concern himself with the opinions of a sheep' to quote George R.R. Martin.

All of a sudden, life was perfect. Yes, I did not have a job at MLS *yet*; heck, I was still seven years away from graduating from university! But something inside of me was clear that I had found my future employer. Because I knew that the league offered the perfect platform for me to create a career in the football industry.

Why am I sharing this story?

Because I genuinely believe that the universe works in a logical way though it may not seem obviously logical to most.

But wanting something cannot be from the head; it must be from the heart, which activates every cell in your body to scream for it. My heart and body were yearning for a job in a company that I knew nothing about, but the want was genuine, and the universe conspired to help me achieve it.

'Follow your heart and make it your decision.'
— Mia Hamm

## The Power of Conviction

It was the summer of 1999.

I was interning at the Hyundai North America headquarters in Fountain Valley, California. The internship was courtesy of my father's employment at this organization and the employee-benefits programme, which provided internship positions for the college-aged offspring of any employee of Hyundai. I was happy to get my first taste of corporate life, as up until then, I had only worked in water parks, restaurants, retail outlets and a university. Ironically, I was placed in the accounting department and spend the first few weeks of my internship entering data into Microsoft Excel sheets for seven hours a day.

In addition to data entry, I spent the first half of the day dreaming about lunch, and after lunch, I spent the next few hours dreaming about completing my shift and going home. I knew that the Microsoft Excel experience I was gaining would be useful for the rest of my life, which it has been. Was I fulfilled or enjoying my work?

*No!*

Since it was just for a summer, I did not want to rock the boat too much, as the last thing I wanted was for my father to lose face with his colleagues thanks to his self-entitled son. Towards the third week of my internship, the HR manager and gatekeeper of the internship programme, Tom Dell, scheduled one-on-one meetings with each of the interns as a general check-in. I decided that I was not going to complain, but would be as honest as possible. After all, it was my life and it was ending every minute …

This opportunity was divine providence because the conversation was life-changing.

Tom said, 'Hi, Neel, how are you enjoying your time at Hyundai?'

'Hello, Mr Dell. First of all, I want to thank you for creating this opportunity to work at Hyundai. It has only been a few weeks, and I've learned a lot from my supervisor and from the work I'm doing. It's not exactly the type of work that I see myself doing once I graduate from university; however, I know that working with one of the top automobile companies in the world is a valuable experience.'

'That's great, Neel. So, what type of work would you like to do once you graduate?'

'Well, my dream is to work for Major League Soccer one day as I'd like to help people grow through football in the way that I did. I know that Hyundai is an automobile company, but I also know that it sponsors US Soccer. I wanted to see if, by any chance, you knew anyone in US Soccer you could introduce me to.'

Tom smiled and replied, 'Wow! I can do even better than that. As you know, the 1999 FIFA Women's World Cup is taking place this summer. And our company is thinking of organizing a community service event for underprivileged kids to have the opportunity to take part in a world-class football training programme and attend the FIFA World Cup Final in LA. I can talk to our marketing department to see if you can join the team working on this project.'

My jaw dropped.

'Yes, yes, yes! This sounds incredible. Thank you, Mr Dell!'

I left the conversation more floating than walking. *How on earth did this happen?* I thought to myself. There I was all geared up to work for a car company the whole summer as a promise that I made to my father for allowing me to spend my third year of university studying in London. And then I was working with the possibility of joining the marketing team of a US Soccer sponsor and having the opportunity to create an event that helps youth grow through the beautiful game. This was precisely what I wanted.

> 'You are the masterpiece
> of your own life.
> You are the Michelangelo
> of your own life.
> The David you are sculpturing
> is you.'— Joseph Vitale (*The Secret*)

Tom moved quickly. The next day, I found myself sitting in a boardroom with Hyundai executives conceptualizing a four-day football camp that would be led by a famous women's football personality. Until a day ago, I was punching thousands of numbers into a Microsoft Excel sheet alone for multiple hours a day. I was now planning a project with a team made up of dynamic individuals across the marketing, community relations and public relations departments. Also, travelling around Orange County visiting football pitches to identify a place where we could host the camp. And meeting with youth organizations to select the beneficiaries of the programme in addition to having daily calls with representatives from US Soccer. All of this was the result of one five-minute conversation. The world was suddenly rich with possibility.

Our words can create worlds. But this is only possible when our outer self is consistent with what our inner self truly wants. At that point, I had spent a little over four years focused on creating a career in the football industry. This was done through multiple conversations with people working in sports, securing after-school employment with the sports department at UC Santa Barbara and reading as many books on sports management that I could get my hands on. So it was no surprise that through just a few sentences, a new world opened up for me, which was in line with what I wanted.

'It only seems impossible until it's done.'
— Nelson Mandela

Many years later when I bumped into Tom, I asked him what made him take me seriously. He said, 'It was not what you said, Neel, it was your conviction and clarity with which you said it that made me want to create the opportunity for you.'

## Happiness Is *Always* an Inside Job

After those first few weeks of surviving through hours of data entry, I reconnected with my best self while organizing the football project with US Soccer. I found myself going to bed at night early, excited to wake up fresh so that I could get a jump-start on my day and continue working off the comprehensive project checklist. I was thinking about the programme non-stop and continuously coming up with new ideas on ways to make it better. I was reaching out to others working in sports to get support and spending every minute I could researching best practices in sports camp programming.

Was this a new me?

*Yes!*

For the first time in my life, I was not waiting for someone to tell me what to do, nor was I trying to 'look good'. I was purely focused on making the project a success because of the impact it could have on hundreds of football-loving youth. My positivity and energy levels remained high, which spread into my personal life as well, as the inner glow of fulfilment served as a magnet for people. I found my dinner-table conversations with my folks to be more loving and animated. I would express and engage with my friends in a brand new way. And I entered into a special romantic relationship as a result of this contagious joy. I was feeling alive.

I worked hard throughout the summer and ended up getting promoted to project lead of the Hyundai Motor America Soccer Camp. I have to admit that the other interns were quite envious, as most of them were still in the state where they were either eagerly awaiting their lunch break or dreaming of going home each day of the week. Thankfully, I was able to bring over a few of them into the project to help with operations. This made me feel less guilty about speaking about my professional transition from cubicle to football pitch whenever we all met for lunch ...

'A great leader's courage to fulfil his vision comes from
passion, not position.' — John C. Maxwell

The Hyundai Motor America Soccer Camp was a massive
success, and the perfect way to complete my first corporate
internship experience. Five hundred youth from Santa Ana,
California, experienced four days of intense football training
under the instruction of local coaches and US Women's
national team player Kristine Lilly. The event was attended
by all the senior management of Hyundai Motor America,
including the CEO. The best part was that all 500 participants
received their own pair of brand new Nike football boots in
addition to a US Soccer uniform. I clearly remember the last
day of the camp when we were handing out the gifts to the
participants. The smiles on the children's faces magically wiped
out my exhaustion caused by sleepless nights, endless amounts
of manual labour and four days running around in the hot
Southern California sun.

'Do not wait until the conditions are perfect to begin.
Beginning makes the conditions perfect.' — Alan Cohen

A few days after the camp, the HR department organized
a post-event party, and I was asked to give a speech to wrap
up the whole project. I was very nervous. Until that point,
the only speeches I had ever given were to my classmates
at school. Now there I was, wearing a suit and tie, standing
at a podium inside the banquet hall of the North America
headquarters for one of the world's biggest automobile
companies and looking out at a hundred people. A group
made up of senior management, the entire internship cohort
and my father. For a split second, I wished that I was safely

back in my cubicle in the accounting department entering numbers into Microsoft Excel.

I had written a speech, but ended up speaking from my heart, sharing how grateful I was to each person who worked on the project. I talked about the participants of the camp and how, thanks to Hyundai's commitment to community development, 500 youth were given an experience of a lifetime and sports equipment that they would be able to use for years to come. I ended by sharing my own story and how football had transformed me from an insecure little boy to a confident young man. And how I am ready to commit my life to create programmes for people all over the world to have the opportunity to experience a similar transformation.

I walked back to my seat to a standing ovation and finally got the courage to glance at Dad. I could clearly see the look of pride all over his face. It was a high I had never experienced before, one that makes me smile and gives me goosebumps even today.

That summer at Hyundai helped me validate and firm up my belief that I would not only enjoy working in the football industry, that I would be good at it as well. There was nothing wrong with the work that I was doing in the accounting department. It would have been a dream job for someone with an analytical mind or who loved numbers. Or for someone who could better connect with the larger picture around how those Excel sheets impact Hyundai's ability to create better automobiles to serve its customers, the country and the world.

'It is better to engage in one's own occupation, even though one may perform it imperfectly, than to accept another's occupation and perform it perfectly.'
— Bhagavad Gita 18.47

## Create Your Reality

If that life-changing conversation with Tom Dell had not happened, I would have most likely continued in the accounting department over the summer and worked hard to impress my boss and my father. And then, when the internship ended, add 'any job where the majority of the work is on Microsoft Excel' to the list of jobs that I do not want to have as a career which, at that point, included lifeguard, shoe salesman, waiter and department store floor runner.

I am all for working hard, putting in the hours, hustling, whatever you want to call it. I just feel that the efforts are at their best when channelized in the right matter. Your professional scope of work should be a natural extension of yourself. There is no point in 'seeing how things pan out' in this area. This typically involves giving into pressure, internal or external, and ending up in a space that does not offer any fulfilment. The deeper we go inside that space, the harder it is to get out.

So, I invite you to do the work early in life. Ask yourself these critical questions to identify your passion, superpower and purpose. See what comes up and then begin to take action in a direction that is aligned with who you are. Each step that you take in your right, self-guided direction reveals so much while creating a new reality. One that did not look possible just a small step ago. I can say this with complete confidence as my whole life is a reflection of this idea.

> 'Follow your bliss and the universe will open
> doors where there were only walls.'
> — Joseph Campbell

# 7

# How I Landed My Dream Job

*Is It Possible to Make Your Dream a Reality?*

## My Mission Statement—My Lifeline

The year was 2002.

I was standing outside Grand Central Station on a cold and windy November afternoon, especially for a boy from Southern California. But I simply did not care.

*Why?*

Because I was lost in my vision. I was staring across the street at the midtown Manhattan office that was home to the MLS league office, the place I have been dreaming about working at since I was fifteen years old when I happened to read about its launch on the front page of the *LA Times*. The address was etched in my memory as I had sent multiple letters to its HR department for almost three years, praying that I would get a shot at a summer internship. The letters were unanswered. Maybe the league was not interested in taking on an intern with limited sports experience who had not yet graduated from university.

As I stood there in a trance, staring at the building, watching people walk outside onto the busy street buzzing with bright yellow taxis, I imagined myself as an MLS employee, heading out to lunch with a colleague as we discussed the new marketing campaign for the league. The imagery is so real that I can feel it in my bones and throughout my cells. I had driven across the country with all my belongings and taken out a hefty education loan to get my MBA in sports management at Seton Hall University, New Jersey, for one big reason: the institute was just a thirty-minute train ride from the MLS league office.

So there I was, twenty-two years old, staring at the building that housed my dream job, not knowing how I would literally and figuratively 'get my foot in the door'. Then, without any thought, I reached into my pocket, pulled out my cell phone and dialled 212-450-1200. It is the phone number to the MLS main line, a number that I had memorized, but never called. My heart started beating fast, and my head was screaming, 'Hang up! Hang up now!' but I did not, and then through my phone, I heard a voice:

'Hello, Major League Soccer, how can I help you?'

'Yes, hello, my name is Neel Shah, and I'm calling because I'd like to enquire about an internship position at MLS.'

'The best way is to apply online at www.mlsnet.com.'

'Yes, I've sent a few letters and applied online but didn't get a response, so I thought I would call directly.'

'Okay, sorry that you didn't hear back, however, I'm not sure what I would be able to do, as our standard application process is online or through a letter.'

'I understand. It is just that I've been dreaming about working for MLS since I was fifteen. Over the last seven years, I have tried to learn as much as possible about football development and marketing with the intention to serve MLS and help grow football in the United States. I have even moved across the country to pursue an MBA in sports management to get closer to the league office. I would appreciate it if I can speak to someone in the marketing department who could guide me on the best way to get an opportunity to serve the league.'

(Long pause.)

'Wow, I've been working the front desk at MLS for three years, and no one has shared something like this before. Let me see what I can do. (Another long pause.) Okay, I'm transferring your call to Mark Noonan, the executive vice president of marketing. Good luck, Neel.'

(I could hear her smile.)

'Hello, this is Mark.'

'Hello, Mark, my name is Neel Shah, and I'm enquiring about an internship opportunity at MLS.'

'It's nice to talk to you, Neel. Our receptionist recommended that I speak with you. So what makes you think you would be a good MLS intern?'

'Mark, my mission in life is to contribute to the growth of football in the United States. The sport has done so much for me, and I just want others to also grow through this beautiful game.'

'That sounds nice, Neel. But I'll ask again, what makes you think that you would be a good MLS intern?'

'Over the past seven years, I've committed myself to learning and experiencing as much as I can to prepare myself to excel at a position in MLS's marketing department. I've organized a football camp for a large international company. I've worked in the sports department at UC Santa Barbara for three years. And during my year studying abroad in London, I spent several weekends attending lower division football matches, trying to understand the emotional relationship between supporters and their favourite clubs. I feel that I can combine my mission with my experience and contribute to MLS achieving its objectives.'

'Wow! Our receptionist was right; you are passionate! Unfortunately, the marketing department does not have any internship positions open right now. However, I believe the special events department may need an intern. I'll speak to Geoff Hayes, the vice president of special events, and he will give you a call to set up an interview.'

'Thank you very much for your time and support, Mark. I look forward to hearing from Geoff and hope to see you in the office soon.'

I hung up and stood silently staring at the same place across the street. My heart was still pumping hard, but a huge smile had taken over my face. *Did this just happen? Am I going to get an interview for an internship position with MLS?* Three years of sending unanswered letters and emails, and all it took was *one* phone call to get an interview? However, deep down, I knew what happened. It was not just luck. Well, some luck, of course. *The positive conversation resulted from years of self-reflection, understanding who I am and what I wanted and taking steps in the direction of my dream job.*

'The only time you run out of chances is when you stop taking them.'— David Beckham

While I might have seemed calm, collected and focused during my conversations with Tom at Hyundai and Mark at MLS, my natural self was quite nervous around people in positions of authority. I tended to shrink and either fumbled my words or spoke too fast. I always put too much pressure on myself to make the most of these interactions and sometimes ended up coming across as uncomfortable or trying too hard. However, that is the beauty of identifying and practising your mission statement. It is this tool that you can tap into at any time, especially during conversations with individuals who can open doors towards the direction of your dreams. Through clarity, conviction and practice, your narrative will come across as natural and will typically leave an impression with the person or persons on the other side.

## How I Achieved 100 Per Cent Motivation on a Monthly Stipend of $0

It was March 2003.

I was into the third month of my internship with the special events department of MLS (yes, I got the internship). Over the past ten weeks, I had worked on a beach football tournament in Miami, created an event plan for the season launch of MLS FirstKick and started building out the strategy for the MLS Fanfest that was to take place alongside the 2003 Pepsi MLS All-Star Game. A game that will be hosted at the newly built Home Depot Center in Carson, California, thirty minutes away from where my folks lived.

I knew that I was living my dream, but it would not look like that to someone on the outside. I would wake up at 6:30 a.m. in South Orange, New Jersey, walk two miles through snow, rain, wind, sleet, etc., to the train station to take the 7:30 a.m. Midtown Direct to Penn Station, fight my way on to a train going uptown to Times Square, where I get the shuttle to Grand Central Station. I would then walk across the street to the MLS office, take the elevator to the tenth floor, say 'hi' to the receptionist, who I am forever indebted to, and walk over to my cubicle.

The next eight hours were full of meetings, meetings and more meetings where I would be taking notes, writing reports, working on project plans and following up with colleagues, club officials, vendors, etc. Then by 5:30 p.m., I would head back to New Jersey the same way I came, walk two and a half miles to my university campus and grind through my MBA classes until 11p.m. After my classes got over, I would walk home and crash by midnight just to wake up and do it all over again the next day. Oh, and in between, I was working on MBA assignments and completing my required readings in addition to travelling to MLS events on the weekends.

This was not an easy time. I was physically exhausted and mentally drained and, at that time, too busy to take stock of how I was doing emotionally. Less than a year ago, I was in California cruising through my final semester at UC Santa Barbara, spending mornings in class and afternoons on the beach. But in New Jersey, I was busy commuting to New York and back, in bone-chilling weather, trying to juggle a rigorous MBA programme and demanding full-time internship at MLS. Without family or friends nearby to provide support or comfort, there were times when I wanted to quit and fly back to the warmth and comforts of my Southern California life. During those tenuous moments, it was only the remembrance of my journey and the strength of my mission statement that kept me moving forward.

Back then, MLS paid interns a monthly stipend of $0 and, of course, there was no guarantee of a job at the end of the internship period. Actually, in the early days of the league, they had so few employees that they almost assured that you would not get a job after your internship just to set expectations. My family thought I was crazy. By now, most of my friends worked at a 'big five' accounting firm making

$50,000 a year, flying business class around the country and attending fancy liquid lunches. While I am earning no income and eating homemade peanut butter jelly sandwiches for lunch each day because that was all I could make and afford at the time.

But I was living an authentic life—working hard, staying positive and feeling fulfilled, which showed up in my attitude and performance at work. And that is what made it worthwhile.

## My First Dream Job

It was two weeks before my twenty-third birthday. I was sitting at my desk working on the MLS All-Star Game Fanfest promotional plan when an email popped up in my inbox. The subject said, 'Internal Announcement—Job Posting'. I quickly opened it and saw the job description for a position called 'coordinator – fan development'. As I started reading the job description, I realized that this was, in fact, my dream job. Every role and responsibility was directly aligned with what I wanted to do, not just at MLS; this was exactly what I wanted to do in my professional life. It felt like a miracle.

This was it!

This position was not just for me. *It was me*! I quickly applied and eventually interviewed with the department head, David Wright; the vice president of marketing and special events, Dianne Lynch; executive vice president of marketing and special events, Mark Noonan; and the head of human resources, Kristina Maloney. It was a gruelling process. During that week, I saw five other people from within and outside MLS go through interviews for the same position, which triggered my insecurities immensely.

Because I was just an intern unlike the other candidates who, at the time, were already working for NFL, NBA and MLS clubs. During that period, I could barely sleep a few hours each night out of anxiety, and when I finally managed to doze off, I would only dream about the moment I was offered the position.

It was 18 March 2003.

It was my twenty-third birthday, and just another day in the office. The word around the cubicles was that the interviews were concluded a few days earlier and that the marketing team was still deciding whom to hire. I was anxious, sleep-deprived and trying my best to remain focused on my special events work although I could not help but think about the position. Then I heard my name called out from one of the offices, 'Neel, can you come over here?' It was Dianne Lynch. I quickly got up from my seat and walked over to her office. (Okay, almost ran to her office.) She was sitting with David Wright and Geoff Hayes.

David asked, 'Hey Neel, how far is your parent's home from San Diego, California?'

'It's about two hours' drive south from my parents's house.'

'Well, let them know that you will be seeing them next week.'

'Why?'

I was clearly very confused.

'Well, our *new* coordinator of fan development needs to travel to California for the American Youth Soccer Organization (AYSO) convention.'

'What? Wait? What? *I got the job?*'

'Yes, congratulations Neel, you are our coordinator of fan development. Welcome to MLS!' said Dianne.

I was speechless. I hugged each of them.

David said, 'You earned it, buddy. Now go and call your parents.'

I immediately left the room, took the elevator down to the ground floor, walked onto the pavement across from the same place I stood while making the cold call to the MLS front desk a few months ago and called Mom and Dad. I broke the good news and told them that I would be seeing them in a week so that we could celebrate in person. I hung up and thought about the significance of what has just happened.

I reflected on my dream job journey starting at Jim's office in 1995; to the conversation with Tom Dell; to years of working in the sports division at UC Santa Barbara; to my research on football fandom while studying in London; to my road trip across the United States to get to the East Coast and be geographically closer to MLS; to all the conversations, dreams and sharing from my heart over the years … and just broke down crying. The seed that I planted in Jim's office in 1995 and watered for years finally blossomed into a beautiful rose bush. This remains one of the most precious moments of my life.

'Hope is a dangerous thing. Hope can drive a man insane.'
— Stephen King

## Never Underestimate a Good Mission Statement

For Paras, his journey to step on to his dream career pathway was not so dramatic. There were no sleepless nights, no tears, no driving across the country, or creepily staring at his future office building from across the street. Through career creation coaching, he recognized that he wanted to work in events management and enrolled in an event planning executive course at Long Beach State University. They were night classes so that he could continue working in his day job 'to pay the bills'.

After completing the course, he shared his mission statement with everyone who would listen while simultaneously applying for every events position in Southern California. It was not easy. Due to his inability to find his path when he was younger, he had not graduated from university, nor did he have any professional work experience in the field of events. To make up for this, he started spending his weekends volunteering at as many events as possible. He also continued to craft and evolve his mission statement until he landed an interview with one of the world's leading and most respected NGOs.

He won the management over with his positive attitude, generous nature and passion for events, and was hired to join the team. His role was to organize massive galas, charity golf tournaments, awards ceremonies and other events to assist families that require financial support. At the age of forty-three and after two decades of professional struggles and multiple failures, Paras finally kick-started his dream career pathway. He was happy, fulfilled, excited to go to work each day, and respected by those in and outside his organization—all experiences he never had during any of his earlier professional engagements.

## How to Chase for Your Passion, Not Pension

Avantika's path towards her dream career started with the understanding that, although she was a rising star in the talent and leadership department at the consulting firm, she was not happy. She wanted to use her training in psychology and passion for the arts on a day-to-day basis to have an impact on individuals. Once she became connected with her mission statement, she shared it with close family and friends. This resulted in one of her aunts letting her know about a course in Bengaluru called Foundation Course in Creative and Expressive Arts Therapies (FECAT) hosted by the Studio for Movement Art and Therapies (SMArT). Though she did not know much about this field at the time, she applied for the course as it combined her passion for arts with psychology.

Once she got accepted, she moved to Bengaluru to pursue the programme. While pursuing FECAT, she expanded on the psychology and counselling theory that she learned in her master's programme and learned how to use creative arts to work with individuals and groups for therapy. She got certified as an expressive arts therapist, returned to New Delhi, built a studio called Soul Canvas—Art for Wellness, and began working as a therapist in schools and hospitals. She crafted her practice for a few years and is now one of the leading expressive arts therapists in India, speaking at international conferences and sitting on the International Expressive Arts Therapy Association board. She is currently living her professional dream. All it took was acknowledging that she was not fulfilled at the consulting firm regardless of the profile and pay, then doing the self-reflection work and taking steps to turn her dream career into a reality.

'Not all those who wander are lost.'— J.R.R. Tolkien

That is the beauty of this process. It guides you so that you know the direction in which you want to walk. It shapes your research, your questions, your answers and your actions. It gives you a sense of clarity and conviction around who you are and what you want to do in the world. And it can lead you to these precious moments, where your dream becomes a reality, the impossible becomes possible, and a whole new world opens up within and around you. These are moments when you can proudly look back and see where you were and the steps that you took despite all challenges to create a new reality.

'If you give up on your dreams, what's left?' — Jim Carrey

# 8

# The Method to Kick-start
# Your Dream Career

*How to Figure Out Your Dream Job(s)?*

'If you don't build your dreams, someone will hire you to help
build theirs.' — Tony Gaskin

## Dream Job or Dream Jobs?

The path to securing my dream job with MLS, Paras
managing events for an NGO and Avantika becoming an
expressive arts therapist was not by chance. There was a
method to the madness, a process that guided our career
conversations and steps which ultimately led us to secure our
respective dream jobs and kick-start our dream careers.

So, what is this process?

How do you go from not having a clue about what you
would like to do professionally to stepping into your dream
job?

I will help you identify the components of the process and take you through how it can work for you in the pursuit of your dream jobs and, ultimately, your dream career.

Yes, you read that right. It is 'jobs' as opposed to 'job'. We all end up having multiple dream jobs because of the various vocations that align with ourselves as we evolve. At any given time, there will be multiple dream jobs available for you to pursue, as a dream job is any position that aligns with your passion, superpower and purpose. Knowing how to always create or secure your dream job is how you achieve a dream career. Fulfilment over your career is easily accessible when your jobs align with these three elements.

The five key components of the process of acquiring your dream job(s) include:

- Checking in
- Identifying key elements of your dream job(s)
- Applying the formula
- Crafting your mission statement
- Taking S-M-A-R-T steps

## Checking In

Life moves fast, and often, we just run alongside without stopping and assessing our situation to see if we are running in the right direction.

*Are you running in the right direction?*

No?

STOP!

Check in with yourself. This ensures that you have some clarity about how you feel about *where you are* and *where you want to go*. It also limits the amount of disempowering thoughts that you bring into the process.

Spend some time in an environment that helps you remain calm and ask yourself the following hard-hitting questions.

- If you are just starting off in your career or not currently working, you can ask:
  - Am I able to see my career as something that is a part of me instead of something I do on the side while living my life?
  - Am I ready to take the steps required to create the best opportunity to enjoy my 100,000 hours?
  - Am I ready to work hard and go through some challenges in order to achieve professional fulfilment?
  - Am I ready to stand strong in what I want in spite of family and societal pressures pushing me in various directions?
  - Do I believe that I can serve society while still earning enough to live a quality life?

- If you are in the middle of a career, you can ask:
  - Does my current job fulfil me?
  - Is my professional scope of work directly aligned with who I am and how I am best suited to serve the world?
  - How much money do I really need to live a quality life?
  - Am I ready to take a road less travelled and, possibly, a road that is not initially supported, in order to create a fulfilling career?

□    Am I willing to do the work required to make professional fulfilment a reality in my life?

Be honest and authentic with your answers. The process
will only be effective if you truly want to experience growth
and fulfilment in your life and are ready do the work to make
it happen. If you sense resistance within yourself while going
through the check-in questions, spend some time reflecting on
the reasons behind it until you feel comfortable with moving
forward. Take the support of someone you trust, a mentor or
a coach if required.

Ready?

## Identifying the Key Elements of Your Dream Job(s)

Without the right ingredients in correct amounts, a dish will
never come out tasty, no matter how good the recipe is.
Similarly, certain critical elements are required to ensure that
your professional life is good as well. As you are well aware
by now, the three magical elements for career fulfilment are
passion, superpower and purpose. To recapitulate:

- *Passion* is a strong liking of something, a hobby, an
  activity, etc., that you like very much; an area of deep
  interest
- *Superpower* is an exceptional or extraordinary ability, a
  unique strength
- *Purpose* is how you want to contribute to the world

I am sharing the self-reflection questions presented earlier
that will help you identify the key factors for your dream job(s),
which will set you on the path towards a dream career. And if

you remember, as in Páras's and Avantika's cases, the answers may not come all at once. It often takes multiple sittings, honest reflection, keen observation of body sensations (like feeling light or energized) and the support of people you trust to solidify what is right for you.

Ask yourself the following questions to discover your passion(s)

- What would I do for free?
- What activities make me feel truly alive or give me a sense of pure joy?
- What activities make me lose track of time?
- What topics do I love to discuss and ponder?
- What in life gives me an irresistible sense of inspiration, a reason to get out of bed?

Ask yourself the following questions to discover your superpower(s):

- What are my strengths?
- What abilities come naturally to me?
- Where do I see the most results in my life? Why?
- What do the people I trust most say I excel at?
- What activities give me energy?
- During what activities am I in the 'flow' or totally absorbed and immersed in my work?

Ask yourself the following questions to discover your purpose in life:

- What is an area of life where I am already contributing and making an impact?

- What do I want the world to have more of?
- What is an area of life that I would like to transform?
- What is something that has significantly impacted my life that I would like to pay forward?
- What is an issue affecting my family, community, state, country, planet, etc., that I want to address?

Why is it important to identify your passion, superpower and purpose? I will explain in the next section.

## Applying the Formula

I have developed a formula to guide people on transforming their passion, superpower and purpose into their dream jobs. I devised this during my tenure at MLS while reflecting on how it was possible that I not only secured my dream job, but also felt deep fulfilment in my role at the league office. An experience that so few people I interacted with could relate to. Here is how it looks:

[(My passion) + (My superpower)] x My purpose = My dream job(s)

Here is how this works:

This is no mathematical formula (you could probably tell from the career options that I immediately rejected in Jim's office that I have limited interest in mathematics). *The formula first helps you to identify some tangible ways to connect your passion with your superpower.* Mainly, get your creative juices flowing as you brainstorm jobs aligned with these two elements. For example, my passion for football and my superpower of getting people interested in or excited about something that has touched, moved or inspired me, when merged, immediately had me thinking about opportunities in the areas of football marketing, football PR, football promotions, etc.

Next, when you multiply your purpose to this combined entity, you start to gain some semblance of clarity around your possible dream job(s). The purpose is the arrow or compass guiding your passion and superpower in the right direction. *Without purpose integrated within, no job can be a dream job.* In my situation, I was working with building awareness around football and creating opportunities for people to grow through football. This led me to explore dream jobs in the areas of football marketing, football programming or community development through football—any role that essentially would allow me to connect these three elements. As you will see in forthcoming chapters, these elements can evolve over time and, to successfully build a dream career, it is essential to ensure that your job(s) always reflect your passion, superpower and purpose no matter how they unfold.

Dream jobs include the types of jobs or roles aligned with *all* the elements of your formula. Typically, the more you get comfortable with the elements of your formula and begin sharing them with people around you, the more clarity you have around your options for dream jobs. Hence, this part is always completed last and does not necessarily need to be identified at the same time as the rest of the elements. That said, if you are slightly impatient like me and feel compelled to write something in this area, you can begin listing some roles or careers that pop into your mind which are aligned with your passion and superpower and then explore how you can align these jobs with your purpose.

While formulae are used to crack tough mathematical problems, this one is more of an art you can (and must) experiment with. Also, remember that focused research and conversations with relevant individuals always help to create more clarity through the process. There is a danger with listing out too many options as that sometimes leads to getting stuck with what you know, which limits the ability for the universe to surprise you. So be comfortable living with your passion, superpower and purpose for some time and observe what begins to emerge with regard to either finding or creating professional opportunities aligned with your elements.

What if you do not want to work for an employer and want to be an entrepreneur? Would the process still work in this scenario?

In fact, the process works best for entrepreneurs, as they do not have to find a way to fit their formulae into the existing job market or create new jobs that align with their formulae. They can simply build their entrepreneurial ventures around their formulae, ensuring that they can monetize the products or services being offered. Also, the mission statement plays a critical role for anyone looking to secure investment for their start-up or to begin building their customer base.

Does this process seem overly complicated or way too simple an approach to guide your career? What is the point of nearly two decades of education only to have a few words to help you figure out how to approach the first or next step in your career, right?

'Education is not the filling of a pail, but the lighting of a fire.'
— William Butler Yeats

I often wondered along these lines as well; however, I truly believe that educational institutions literally and figuratively can serve as playgrounds for humanity. Places where you can gain exposure to various concepts, paths and people while introspecting who you are and where you want to go. It is basically a safe space to push your mental and social limits and test the waters before entering the so-called real world.

> 'Most people work just hard enough not to get fired and get paid just enough money not to quit.'
> — George Carlin

Do *you* want to be one of them?

My formula will serve as a roadmap; it helps you determine where you are heading. Once you have figured this out, everything else essentially becomes more fluid. The formula will guide what you research, whom you reach out to, what questions you ask and what you speak about in your search for a dream career that fulfils you.

## Crafting Your Mission Statement

Once you have understood the formula, the next step is to come up with a mission statement, which represents who you are and what you want to do in the world. It should be clear, concise and strong enough to unlock thick, dead-bolted doors and quiet down the noisiest of well-intentioned, but naive people who are not comfortable with you pursuing a career that is directly in line with your heart. It is not a lofty vision, but a focused mission which can help your formula crack your career dilemma.

Between the five-minute conversation with Tom Dell at the Hyundai Motor America headquarters and the ten-minute phone conversation with the MLS receptionist and Mark Noonan while I stood on a crowded street in Manhattan, my professional life was curated in a way which connected to who I was and where I wanted to go. Fifteen minutes to possibly transform my experience of 100,000 hours. This narrative did not emerge overnight though. You must first believe it, feel it and then practise it over and over again so that when you share it, it leaves an impression on the other person. Your mission statement is not an elevator pitch; no, this is regularly expressing who you are with the world and watching new avenues for action unfold. Understandably, I am a firm believer in the immense power of the mission statement.

I understand that coming up with your mission statement can be daunting, and for some, an impossible exercise. That is the beauty of this work though. It provides you with a framework to self-reflect and finds questions to ask yourself, which will help you unravel what you are interested in, what you are good at and how you would like to contribute to the world. Once this becomes slightly clearer, it is easy to come up with a mission statement that can create new worlds even in unexpected circumstances. Just as I was able to end up working with US Soccer during my internship with an automobile company.

A powerful mission statement:

- reveals something that makes you unique;
- clearly communicates the contribution you want to make in a specific area;
- highlights a few experiences, strengths or skills you possess that align with the difference you intend to make; and
- is honest and convincing.

The following steps will help you to ace the process of crafting an effective mission statement:

1.  Write down your mission statement.
2.  Read it out loud to yourself a few times until you memorize the essence of the words.
3.  Stand in front of a mirror and share it with yourself— check to ensure that you own your words and are not reading a script.
4.  Share your narrative with someone you can trust and get feedback on what they feel about what you are expressing.
5.  Incorporate the feedback (if relevant) and keep on expressing it repeatedly.

Sounds forced? Trust me, it works. The process of getting clear on who you are and what is important to you and being able to share yourself with the world unabashedly is a gift. (That you will cherish for life.) Following through on this exercise can open doors that you may have never even known existed. When someone asks you the question, 'So, what do you want to do in life?', you will be able to confidently answer it with a statement that reflects your authentic self and not you as who you *think* you are or what others may want to hear. Sometimes we get so caught up in answering how we feel we *should* answer that it starts to sound like the truth, which can be destructive on the path of creating your dream career.

## Vision Boards

Once you are set with your mission statement, express it to anyone who will listen. The more you share it, the more doors will open and the more the universe will work to manifest what you want. This is just a reality, *words can create worlds*, and you must share the world you have created within yourself to ensure that it shows up on the outside. If you want to support this process, create a vision board of images representing these dream jobs and put it up in a place where you will often see it. I am a big believer in the power of manifestation, and it is something that I highly recommend you explore making a regular practice in your life. Vision boards are a collection of images or objects arranged in a way to help you manifest your goals or vision. Nearly every future of mine was already created as a collage of images on a poster board in my room, long before becoming a reality.

## Taking S-M-A-R-T Steps

As mentioned earlier, there is no such thing as original thought, only original action. Focused action is required to turn the formula into an actual dream job. And the first step in that direction is to make a to-do list.

The list will include activities that ensure you are regularly engaging in creating your dream job. And the value of each step is different. For some of you, it could be as small as researching the area of a dream job or sharing a mission statement with your family and friends. For others, it may be as big as building a website or taking a trip to a new country to expand their knowledge and network. Please ensure that you are engaged in such kind of activities daily to stay highly motivated and energized. Also, find ways to acknowledge and reward yourself as you complete the steps. Make it fun!

'The only place success comes before work is in the dictionary.' — Vince Lombardi

For those of you who like to make vague, lofty to-do lists that never get completed, I recommend that you come up with S-M-A-R-T steps to make your list.

- S = Specific
  - □ State what you will do
  - □ Use action words
- M = Measurable
  - □ Provide a way to evaluate
  - □ Ensure you can clearly tell whether the step has been completed or not
- A = Achievable
  - □ Within your scope
  - □ Possible to accomplish, attainable
- R = Relevant
  - □ Is aligned with your formula
  - □ Makes sense
- T = Time-bound
  - □ State when you will get it done
  - □ Be specific on date or time frames

Once you take the S-M-A-R-T steps, it will raise your confidence, motivation and enthusiasm and will open up new realities that did not exist in your mind when you started the process. Half of this work has to do with creating positive progress in the world as you move towards securing your dream job, and the other half of the work has to do with your mind. It is important to believe that you not only deserve, but also are capable of creating a dream career. You must believe that you are *worthy* and *able* to make your dream job a reality and, trust me, every accomplishment will provide the emotional and mental fuel required to continue down the path.

These are the five steps to securing your dream job and getting on the path to enjoying a dream career. Depending on your situation and the results of your formula, it may take days, weeks, months or even years to secure your dream job and build a dream career. Do not let this deter you. *The journey is just as enjoyable as the destination.* Every time you are engaged in activities aligned with your passion, superpower and purpose, you will be nourishing your mind, body and spirit in some way. Also, often, just the knowledge that you are in the process of creating something new for your future or paving a path that will move you out of a 'stuck' professional situation offers some mental peace—especially during those dark phases that tend to creep in from time to time.

'Don't give up on your dreams, or your dreams will give up on you.' — John Wooden

# 9

## The Dream Jobs Process Proved Successful

*How Does This Work in Real Life?*

'Integrity is a life where your beliefs and intentions are aligned with your words and actions.' — Stephen Lovegrove

The process laid down by me is powerful and effective if you understand and properly follow it with an open mind and sincere commitment to generate professional fulfilment in your life. In this chapter, I will share how Paras's, Avantika's and my processes looked before you begin to work on your own. My process was completed in hindsight while reflecting on my career journey, while Avantika and Paras came up with theirs through focused career creation sessions.

### My Process

- *Checking In (what came up when I answered some of the checking-in questions)*

- □ 'I do not want a position working in banking, business analysis or accountancy.'
- □ 'I've had so many jobs that I don't like and definitely do not want just to survive in my career.'
- □ 'I want to work in an area of life that I am passionate about, and right now, I'm only really passionate about football.'
- *Key Elements*
  - □ Passion: Football.
  - □ Superpower: Get people interested in or excited about something that has touched, moved or inspired me.
  - □ Purpose: To create opportunities for people to grow through football.
- *Formula*
  - □ [(Passion: Football) + (Superpower: Get people interested in or excited about something that has touched, moved or inspired me)] x Purpose: To create opportunities for people to grow through football =
    - ○ Aligned Jobs (Passion + Superpower).
      - ▪ Marketing role with a broadcaster that airs football matches on television (i.e., ESPN).
      - ▪ PR role for a football league or team.
      - ▪ Sports journalist with a focus on football news and events.
    - ○ Possible Dream Jobs (when purpose is included).
      - ▪ Marketing or community development role for a professional football league or team.
      - ▪ Marketing role with a youth football administrative organization (i.e., American

> > Youth Soccer Organization, US Youth Soc-
> > cer, US Club Soccer).
>
> - Programming role for a non-profit focused
>   on contributing to society through foot-
>   ball.

- *Mission Statement*

'The sport of football has profoundly impacted my life and has contributed to my growth—emotionally, physically and socially. I would like to pay this forward and am fully committed to creating opportunities for people to benefit from this beautiful game. I have taken steps to strengthen my ability to do this through years of football-related internships and by pursuing an MBA in Sports Management. I am now ready to take on a professional role in football marketing. My unwavering commitment combined with my experience and education, will provide me with what I require to excel in any role connected to creating awareness for the sport.'

- *S-M-A-R-T Steps*

1. Research all positions in the United States related to football marketing; make a list with contact information.
2. Set up an informational interview with someone who currently works in football marketing and understands what skills and qualifications are required to get a job in this field.
3. Draft a cover letter which can be customized for football marketing positions.
4. Read a book on sports marketing principles.
5. Research and begin to understand the US football landscape.

6.  Speak with the programme director of Seton Hall University and request her to help set up introductions with anyone working in the professional football industry.

7.  Volunteer to work at America SCORES a non-profit on weekends.

8.  Set up a blog to share my thoughts around football in the United States.

9.  Apply for an internship at MLS.

10. Speak to someone at the MLS league office.

## Paras's Process

- *Checking In (what came up when Paras answered some of the checking-in questions)*
  - 'I know that I'm smart, but why do I always end up in jobs that I don't like.'
  - 'I don't enjoy doing back-end processing jobs where I don't feel stimulated or respected.'
  - 'I'd like to do something more active, be around people and have some fun at work.'

- *Key Elements*
  - Passion: Live events.
  - Superpower: Organizing engaging experiences for people.
  - Purpose: Making people happy.

- *Formula*

[(Passion: Live events) + (Superpower: Organizing engaging experiences for people)] x Purpose: Making people happy =

- ○ Aligned Jobs (Passion + Superpower)
  - ▪ Private events planner.
  - ▪ Part of an events management agency staff.
  - ▪ Part of the events department for a professional sports organization.
  - ▪ Organizing events for a non-profit.
- ○ Possible Dream Jobs (when purpose is included)*
  - ▪ Private events planner.
  - ▪ Part of an events management agency staff.
  - ▪ Part of the events department for a professional sports organization.
  - ▪ Organizing events for a non-profit.

* In Paras's case, his aligned jobs were the exact same as his possible dream jobs options which can happen.

- *Mission Statement*

'I have organized events my entire life, for family, friends, communities and have always succeeded in creating safe, engaging environments where people can have fun and connect. I am deeply committed to spreading joy in the world by producing unique, memorable and impactful events. My experience in this area combined with the learnings from my recent events planning course, make me a suitable candidate for any positions in the events space.'

- *S-M-A-R-T Steps*

1. Research all event management companies in Southern California; make a list with contact information.
2. Continue work with the Long Beach Junior Chamber of Commerce.

3. Request the president of the Long Beach Junior Chamber of Commerce to support with helping me find a job with an events company.

4. Spend two weekends a month volunteering at local events.

5. Update resume to include events planning course as well as volunteer experience.

6. Research NGOs that are looking for people to hire within the events space.

7. Contact all local family and friends, letting them know that I am offering my services to organize an event for them or someone in their circles.

8. Create a cover letter that can be customized for event positions.

9. Reach out to people who work in events and set up informational interviews with them.

10. Shortlist companies and start applying.

## Avantika's Process

- *Checking In (what came up when Avantika answered some of the checking-in questions)*
  - 'While I am pleased with the fact that I have a job with a top multinational company and get to work with big clients, I am completely missing the human interaction and impact element in my day-to-day work.'
  - 'I studied psychology for many years but don't feel like I'm getting the opportunity to integrate my education with my work.'
  - 'I love the arts and would like to find a way to bring the arts into my professional life.'

- *Key Elements*
  - Passion: Expressive arts.
  - Superpower: Making people feel at ease in my presence.
  - Purpose: Creating spaces for people to heal and feel empowered.
- *Formula*

[(Passion: Expressive arts) + (Superpower: Making people feel at ease in my presence)] x Purpose: Creating spaces for people to heal and feel empowered =

- Aligned Jobs (Passion + Superpower)
  - Art teacher
  - Street artist
  - Professor of Fine Arts
- Possible Dream Jobs (when purpose is included)
  - Expressive arts facilitator
  - Expressive arts therapist
  - Expressive arts studio owner

- *Mission Statement*

'I am deeply committed to empowering and healing people through the medium of the arts. And I am confident that given my training in psychology and expressive arts therapy, my life-long engagement with the arts, and my presence and ability to actively listen to others, I would excel in any field that involves helping people express and grow through the arts.'

- *S-M-A-R-T Steps*

1. Identify organizations that would be open to alternative forms of education and therapy.

2. Approach schools, hospitals and non-profit organizations to conduct training workshops using expressive arts therapy as a medium.
3. Host expressive arts therapy sessions in public forums.
4. Speak to parents about turning their basement into an expressive arts studio.
5. Identify people currently working in the field of expressive arts therapy and set up informational interviews with them.
6. Volunteer at hospitals and non-profit organizations on weekends to get some experience with using art to heal and empower individuals and groups.
7. Build an online presence showcasing work and creating awareness.
8. Update resume to include any work connected to expressive arts therapy and psychology.
9. Participate in relevant networking conferences and events.
10. Let all family and friends know that I am exploring career opportunities in areas that connect arts and healing.

## Exercise

'Get out of your head and get into your heart.
Think less, feel more.' — Osho

*The key to the process of finding your dream job and creating a dream career is to move from your head to your heart.*

This is the time to go deep within and find out what you truly want for yourself and your life. And, most importantly, do not get caught up in the how or focus on logistics and practicalities at this stage in the process.

Here are a few suggestions on how to create a space within and around yourself that will allow for your authentic self to emerge:

- Be in an environment that has either peaceful or inspiring/aspirational energy.
- Ensure that you are alone and will not be disrupted, especially during the first time you go through this exercise.
- Turn off all electronic devices.
- Take a few deep breaths or meditate for at least five minutes before beginning the process.
- Remain in a space of possibility, believing that anything you want can become a reality.

You can now recreate the simple template below in a notebook, journal, electronic document or whiteboard and begin the process.

*Checking In*
- ' _____ '
- ' _____ '
- ' _____ '

*Key Elements of My Dream Job*
- My Passion(s): _____
- My Superpower(s): _____
- My Purpose(s): _____

*My Dream Jobs Formula*

[(Passion:_____) + (Superpower:_____)]
x Purpose: _____ =

- My Aligned Jobs (Passion + Superpower)
  - ▫ _____
  - ▫ _____
  - ▫ _____

- My Possible Dream Jobs (when purpose is included)
  - ▫ _____
  - ▫ _____
  - ▫ _____

*My Mission Statement*

_____

_____

_____

_____

_____

_____

*S-M-A-R-T Steps (I recommend that you try to identify at least ten such steps)*

1. _____
2. _____
3. _____
4. _____
5. _____
6. _____

7. _____

8. _____

9. _____

10. _____

It is essential to understand that the initial session will more than likely not give you the clarity you are looking for, which is completely fine. It is a starting block, a point to kick-start your journey towards creating a fulfilling career. Imagine you are planning a dream holiday with a friend or partner. You would need to spend some time identifying what you want from the holiday: relaxation, adventure, cultural experiences, etc., before you finalize where you are going. So, consider that you are planning a 100,000-hour journey with the most important person, *yourself*, and you must remain patient as you explore where you want to go and why.

'Faith is taking the first step even when you don't see the whole staircase.' — Martin Luther King Jr

# 10

# My Giant Leap Forward

*What Happens When Your Dream Job Is No Longer a Dream?*

## How the 'Hero' Got Rescued

It was December 2006.

I was in Gujarat, India, sitting in the same home where Dad lived from 1942 to 1950. Kashipura, a village just thirty kilometres outside Vadodara, comprised mostly of farmers living off their crops and cattle.

It was my first trip to India, and this visit was one of the highlights of my two-and-a-half-week itinerary across the country where my parents spent their youth. I remember months earlier receiving an email from Saroj Foi, my paternal aunt living in Vadodara, confirming that she would take me to Kashipura during my short stay in Gujarat. I laid down on my bed in Brooklyn, New York, and pictured the following scene:

*The handsome hero from the United States strides into the poor Indian village and is greeted with garlands, sweets and fruits. The village men cannot wait to befriend this exotic foreign hunk, and the women just blush whenever they are around him. He wows the villagers with stories about the West and motivates them with inspiring phrases like 'follow your heart' and 'impossible is nothing'. Finally, just before leaving, the successful sports marketing executive hands over a bag of cash to the village headman, ensuring that all the kids in the village will have sports equipment to play with for the next few years. The whole village starts dancing in unison to celebrate this generous gift. The hero then departs in his chauffeur-driven car and the villagers run behind the vehicle, waving and smiling until they fade off into the distance.*

This was the kind of ridiculous and cheesy Bollywood-or possibly Hollywood-style scene that I imagined would occur when I arrived in my ancestral village. Instead, my aunt, cousins and I just drove into the village and wandered around until we found Dad's childhood home, still in the same condition it was when they left in 1950. We knocked on the door, and a gentle-looking woman opened it. My aunt explained to her in Gujarati that she lived in the same house when she was a young girl, as did my father. And that we had driven over from Vadodara to see the village and, hopefully, the home. The woman graciously invited us in, pulled up some chairs and there we were sitting in a small circular area with eleven members of their family. They were occupying the three beds located in the centre of the drawing room.

Although there were no garlands, sweets or fruits or envious men and blushing women, I still thought I could help them. In my mind, I was a symbol of success. Highly educated, working in midtown Manhattan, living in the 'cool' part of Brooklyn, director-level designation, good salary and an experienced world traveller. Standing there in the room drinking overly sweet Indian tea and munching on Parle-G biscuits, I started going through the different ways I could be the hero. Suddenly, this train of thought was interrupted by a series of questions from the curious elder of the family. He was a farmer with a walking stick, deep wrinkles, soft eyes, bright smile, no teeth and a mustache to die for. I spoke in short, simple sentences because I had a limited vocabulary while speaking in Gujarati:

The farmer asked, 'How is your father?'

'He's good, uncleji.'

'Where do you live?'

'New York City.'

'You live with your parents?'

'No'

'Then where do your parents live?'

'They live in California.'

'How far is that from where you live?'

'About six hours away, uncleji.'

(Two hands on steering wheel motion.)

'By driving?'

(I moved my flat right hand in a forward and upward motion.)

'By airplane.'

'So you live with your wife and children?'

'No, I don't have a wife or children.'

(His smile slowly faded.)

'So whom do you live with?'

'I live alone.'

(Smiling less now.)

'Who cooks food for you?'

'I eat most of my meals in restaurants.'

(He was frowning now.)

'You live alone and so far from your parents and eat most of your meals outside your home?'

'Yes, uncleji.'

I looked up, and it was not only the farmer who was frowning; it was the other ten people on the beds as well. Did I say something wrong? Although I was not too proficient at speaking Gujarati, I was pretty sure that I did not slip and say a curse word or something disrespectful during that short interrogation. The family huddled together for a few moments, and then the oldest woman of the household whispered into my aunt's ear, who immediately tried to suppress laughter with tears starting to well up in her eyes. She pulled me aside and said, 'Neel, this family feels bad that you live such a hard life, alone and far from your parents. They want to know if you would like to stay here in this house and live with them.'

*They could help me?*

I went through so many emotions at that moment. Here I was thinking about how I could help out these *poor* villagers. But to them, I was a sad ABCD who lived alone and never had home-cooked meals. I was grateful, confused and shaken up by an experience that went in the entirely opposite direction of what I had imagined. Honestly, though, at the time, I had no idea how much that village visit would impact my life.

Life is not meant to be lived as a straight line. We are dynamic beings, and it is vital that we live in accordance with who we are in the moment, wherever that may take us. It is not natural to reach a set destination and then stay there forever. Every moment is a new journey, each minute a new adventure. You can only control the 'now' of life. We must regularly check in with ourselves to ensure we are still living in line with our natural self. This means asking the tough questions, being honest with our answers and always reading the signs presented by the universe. (And I am not talking about aliens here!)

This approach to living certainly holds true when it comes to your career. As I have mentioned earlier, your job should be a natural extension of yourself. It also means that as you evolve, so does your relationship with your career. It does not imply quitting your current job every time you experience personal growth. It is about being aware of how that growth affects your experience of what you are doing professionally and ensuring that there is still alignment. If there is not, it is time to undergo the process. Begin planting seeds to help you prepare for a future shift and start taking some S-M-A-R-T steps to recalibrate your position in your current organization or in the direction of your next dream job.

This concept is at the heart of choosing to live a dream career. It is essential to ensure that your vocation aligns with your evolving formula. Or, at the very least, ensure you are reflecting on what is alive for you and taking appropriate actions to discover and move towards the next phase of your dream career pathway.

'Life will give you whatever experience is most helpful for the evolution of your consciousness.' — Eckhart Tolle

After the Kashipura village awakening, I experienced India through a different lens. I no longer saw myself as the guy who 'made it' and was coming over to India to explore and then return to my comfortable life in New York. I saw India as a place to grow and learn about myself and about a country and culture that was both familiar and foreign. I also let go of the idea that just because I was from the West, I could 'help' people in the East. That notion was silly and not grounded in anything but my ignorance and arrogance. Yes, I wanted to contribute to the people I interacted with while in India, and I wanted to learn from them as well. These learnings came so frequently that I started questioning so much of what I believed to be true by the end of the trip.

## How I Answered to the Call from within

I returned home to a frigid NYC winter in early 2007. As soon as I sat in the yellow taxi outside John F. Kennedy Airport to take me back to my apartment in Brooklyn, I knew that everything had changed. I was the same person physically, but something had shifted within me mentally, emotionally and even spiritually. Suddenly, I did not feel the same high about being promoted to director of the fan development department, making me the youngest director in the MLS league office. I did not see MLS as my forever and, heck; for the first time since I was twenty-two years old, I did not see NYC as the place I would spend the rest of my life. It was a scary time because almost overnight, the future that I had so carefully crafted in my mind started to look less than perfect. Also, this constant thought took over me: *If this isn't my future, then what would it look like?*

We all go through such times when an image of our future that seems so clear, suddenly becomes hazy. Often, for no logical reason at all. While these times could feel like a curse, *they are actually a blessing*. Because it is the universe sending you a sign that an external shift is required to align with the shifts that are taking place internally. This is the time to do the following:

1. Slow down.
2. Become aware of what is going on within you.
3. Do not judge or criticize yourself; just go with it.
4. Reconnect with the process using a clean slate—let go of logistics, obligations or the thought of what people will say.
5. Once you have some clarity, take action.

After the trip, I returned to my office, jet-lagged and full of confused energy. I still loved football, MLS, my colleagues and my projects. However, I could not stop thinking about India. I would regularly reflect on my trip and think about how incredible I felt during some of my meetings with Indian football officials and while playing football with the kids at the various schools I visited. I reminisced about the rush of energy I would feel while riding trains and buses through the country and watching village after village pass. Sitting in my large director's office located in a new building, a skyscraper on 5th Avenue and 37th Street, I could still smell the intoxicating fragrances of Indian food and hear the never-ending array of sounds that filled every space in which I walked while I was traversing the extraordinary country.

I quickly understood that the only way I could stay sane was to go through the process and then take action in the direction of the results. So, once the jet lag wore off, I put on a thick coat, gloves and a scarf and walked over to my favourite bench in Prospect Park. I was going to figure out my next move and rid myself of this confused energy. With *Call of the Mystic* playing on my iPod, I pulled out my notebook and started writing.

[(Passion: Football) + (Superpower: Get people interested in or excited about something that has touched, moved or inspired me)] x Purpose: To create opportunities for people to grow through football (*in India???*) = ...

After doing this work and reflecting, I realized that my formula had not changed at all. That my role as the MLS director of fan development was still aligned with my passion, superpower and purpose. But I could not figure out how and where India would fit into my bigger picture. I wrote 'Indian football' at the top of my notebook and under it, I started writing down the different ways to integrate this topic into my day-to-day life. This is what I came up with:

1.  Spend at least one hour a day researching Indian business, sports, media and entertainment news.
2.  Reach out to at least one Indian football organization a week to build my network.
3.  Offer knowledge sharing services to Indian football stakeholders.
4.  Begin creating programmes for Indian youth footballers in and around New York.
5.  Write an article about my trip and share it with Indian newspapers in the US.
6.  Speak to my network in the US sports community to see if anyone has contacts in the Indian sports industry.
7.  Spend time visualizing myself being a part of the Indian football industry.
8.  Begin learning Hindi.
9.  Take a few MLS executives to lunch at my favourite Indian restaurant and discuss ways to connect MLS with India.
10. Create a system where my friends and family can donate equipment for development through football NGOs in India.

I did not figure out my future in that one sitting in Prospect Park. However, I did become clear that I must include Indian football in my life. And that I had to take certain steps to ensure this happens often, knowing that through focused energy, new avenues for action would continue to show up and new realities would begin to emerge.

'A journey of a thousand miles begins with a single step.'
— Lao Tzu

This is exactly what I did. I spent the next few months focusing on engaging in all ten of the action items I set for myself. I signed up to receive notifications for relevant Indian news stories. I filled many evenings on calls with Indian football executives discussing the landscape and opportunities for me to share knowledge from the US. I regularly started visiting Indian organizations in Queens, New York, to create football programmes for their youth. Everyone who knew me in the football industry knew that I was on a mission to support the development of football in India. I created a vision board filled with pictures of Indian sports and started watching Bollywood films to learn Hindi. I even organized three separate lunch meetings with MLS executives Kathy Carter, Nelson Rodriguez and David Wright at Curry Dreams to discuss MLS and India.

*Outcomes?*

My article titled, '50 Things I Learned in India' was published in a few Hindi and Gujarati publications. My friend Kevin Carroll offered to donate 300 footballs to whichever organizations I chose in India. By June 2007, I was known as the 'Indian football guy' in addition to serving the growth of football in North America through my role as MLS's director of fan development. Then towards the end of 2007, I was invited to travel back to India to spend time with members of the All India Football Federation (AIFF) and other Indian football stakeholders. I gladly accepted, and in December 2007, I flew to India for meetings, to donate Kevin's 300 footballs and for more learnings and adventures. This turned out to be a far more structured trip.

On my first day, I met Sukhvinder Singh, who, at the time, was the director of marketing for the AIFF. My multi-hour conversation with him set the stage for the rest of my two-and-a-half weeks in India. This included meetings with Adidas, Nike, state football associations, grassroots football organizations, schools and NGOs focused on helping kids develop through sport.

I even attended my first professional Indian football match, the Federation Cup final, Mohun Bagan versus Dempo SC in Kolkata's famed Salt Lake Stadium, along with 80,000 raucous supporters. Through some extraordinary circumstances, I missed my flight back to New York, which created an extra day spent with Sukhvinder in New Delhi at the AIFF's 'Football House' and his home. This led to hours of dialogue around Indian football and avenues for me to contribute to the industry—a conversation that set the foundation for the magic that was yet to come.

On the fourteen-hour flight back to NYC, I wrote a detailed report on the past, present and future of football in India and identified where I could support the ecosystem. What started to emerge was that the key stakeholders at the top of the pyramid (Ministry of Youth Affairs and Sports, the federation, multinational companies) wanted football to grow, just as the organizations at the bottom of the pyramid wanted football to grow. However, there were not any platforms, partnerships or programmes that allowed for collaborative and meaningful conversation so that the sport could flourish. This was no different from the situation when I joined MLS in 2003. There was a gap in effective communication between the top and the bottom of the pyramid.

Through the fan development department's activities, we worked hard to close that gap as much as possible. Also, the sporting landscape in both countries were quite similar in that football was not the number one sport. This meant that, as administrators, we had to learn how to build national awareness and relevance for the beautiful game in environments where the general public and media were primarily focused on other sports. And the fact that I was of Indian origin provided me with a sense of connection to the country and a feeling of enthusiasm to 'pay forward' the incredible sporting experiences I had in my life, both on and off the pitch.

By the time I landed in NYC, I had realized something both revealing and powerful: *I was one of the most uniquely positioned people in the world to support the growth of football in India.*

## The Inner Shift

This time, upon returning, I was jet-lagged but *no longer* confused. And it was clear that while my body was in NYC, my head and heart were still in India. The feeling was so intense that it took over me and stuck around no matter how hard I tried to focus on my future at MLS. But I still did not know much about India, and the thought of moving there, at the time, seemed very far-fetched. But how come this feeling was so intense? Then my twelve years of practice of responding to strong signs from within was ignited and, without overthinking, I started taking actions that were in line with my internal feeling and messages.

I scheduled a few long calls with Sukhvinder that ultimately led to a conversation with the Indian office of Dentsu, which, at the time, was one of the world's largest advertising agencies. I had met its sports marketing head, Tarun Chaudhry, at the Federation Cup final. He communicated that he was interested in hiring someone to lead a Dentsu initiative called Goal 11, a national marketing campaign focused on promoting football in India. Over the next few months, along with the president of Dentsu, Rajesh Agarwal, we had a couple of more calls to discuss the project, my ideas, salary, joining date and other perks. I was letting the momentum created by each step feed the next and at no point did the process feel rushed or not in line with my inner self. Then, when the offer letter was emailed by Tarun, that was exactly when things got real.

Imagine, I had dreamed of working for MLS since I was fifteen years old. At twenty-nine, I was the director of the fan development department, respected in the US football industry, making more money than I thought I would make before turning thirty and living in NYC in the same neighbourhood as my best friends. *And I was ready to give it all up to move to India to help Indian football grow.* India, a country where I had spent a total of five weeks, over two glorified backpacking trips and with no comfort with its national language. Also, to join an advertising agency that offered to pay me what will eventually net out to be 15 per cent of what I am currently earning at MLS.

Yes, it was crazy.

But as Neale Donald Walsch puts it, 'Life begins at the end of your comfort zone', my friend.

## Mission Impossible?

*No way!*

Understandably, when I started sharing the news about the offer letter with my most trusted friends and family, they all thought I was mad! The first response was usually, 'Haha; there is no way *you* are moving to India.' But when they would see the seriousness on my face, they would begin to get serious as well. 'No way, you can't move to India! What about your job at MLS? You love that job!' 'Do they even play football in

India?' or 'Is it safe in India, you don't even know the language, how will you get by?'

I did not have answers to most of the questions, but I trusted in the process. So, I just stuck with my mission statement:

*My time developing football in the United States over the past seven years has provided me with invaluable experience and an extensive network that I can tap into to serve the Indian football industry. Also, I have a strong connection with the country and feel driven to create opportunities for people in India to grow through football. This makes me confident that I am uniquely positioned to support the development and promotion of the Indian football ecosystem. Dentsu is offering me an incredible opportunity to do this, and I am ready to take it.*

People could not argue with that. The strength of my mission statement would just shut out their fears. I was reasonably convinced and knew that I could not get everyone on my side right away but that, over time, they would eventually come around.

The weekend after receiving the offer letter, I flew to Los Angeles to speak with my parents. While a part of me thought that they would be proud that I was returning to the country of their roots, the reality turned out to be very different. They were freaked out beyond belief. To them, India represented poverty, crowds, corruption, disease and constant struggle. They were okay with me taking short trips to the country from time to time but were uncomfortable with the idea of me moving there. I heard them out and then basically repeated my mission statement until they had nothing left to throw at me. (*No, not literally.*) Then, when the environment became less tense, I reminded them that they had also freaked out when I said I was going to pursue a career in professional football. This kicked off a whole round of discussions about how different NYC and MLS are from India and Dentsu. Eventually, that argument died down as well, and my parents finally conceded. They said they would support me if I took the job as long as I called them from India at least once a day and visited the United States as much as possible. I happily accepted.

On the flight back to NYC, I pulled up the offer letter on the screen of my laptop, closed my eyes and asked my heart, 'Neel, do you really want to do this? Are you sure you want to resign from MLS and move to India? Everything inside of me screamed, *Yes, let's do it!* I immediately hit 'send' on the email that had been sitting in my drafts folder for about a week, which essentially said that I accept the offer to join Dentsu and will plan to move to New Delhi in October 2009 to begin working on the Goal 11 project. I had the rest of the flight to change my mind, but as soon as I landed at LaGuardia Airport, I logged into the airport internet, and with nervous excitement, I watched the acceptance email leave my outbox.

> 'Have the courage to follow your heart and intuition. They somehow know what you truly want to become.'
> — Steve Jobs

## Resigned from My Job, Not Life

I got back to the office the next day and wrote my letter of resignation. MLS was my first and only full-time professional job up to that point, and I never imagined that I would resign from the dream job that I had worked so hard to get. But then I comforted myself in the knowledge and acceptance that my new dream job was now helping to grow the Indian football landscape. After seven years of building football in North America, I printed out and signed the resignation letter and handed it over to my boss, MLS marketing director Marco Liceaga. It took tremendous courage to do this. Even looking back now, I have no idea how I willed myself to take this final step required to create space for my Indian adventure to begin.

Marco was shocked, as was everyone at the office. They all knew how much I loved MLS and could not believe that I would give it all up to move to India—a cricket-loving country—to work in the football industry there. However, I stuck to my mission statement. Of course, I changed the words up, so that I did not sound like a robot, but the essence of my communication remained the same. And eventually, everyone not only accepted my choice, but I also started receiving incredible words of support and appreciation from so many of my peers working in the US football industry. What was most surprising and endearing though were the people who called to share that my bold decision had helped them find the courage to take steps towards one or more of their dreams.

That is the beauty of following your formula. It not only creates magic in your own life, but also creates a space for others to begin exploring how they can live a life that is in line with their natural selves. Everyone has a dream, something pulling at their heartstrings, urging them to take action. However, most people bury them deep within themselves, writing them off as an irresponsible thought or phase. Then someone around them steps off the beaten path and chooses to create their own road and, all of a sudden, those sensations jump out from the background into the forefront and say, 'See, I told you we can do this!' This is all happening in the subconscious and sometimes even the unconscious mind and is rarely discussed on a day-to-day basis.

'... And as we let our own light shine, we unconsciously give
other people permission to do the same.'
— Marianne Williamson

As a director, I had a month-long notice period, which
turned into a month-long farewell party. It seemed like
everyone connected to football in America wanted to take
me out for drinks and wish me luck on my adventure. It was
embarrassing. There was so much praise, but all I had done up
until then was resign from my position at MLS. Nevertheless, I
thoroughly enjoyed the outpouring of love and respect. I kept
hearing the same phrases: 'You are going to kill it in India',
'Indian football is so lucky to have you', 'You will be the person
who transforms football in India', or 'India will qualify for a
FIFA World Cup with you there'.

## It Is the Journey That Matters, Not the Destination

Then on 24 October 2009, I took two bags and all the
encouragement, letters and cards with me on my flight from
New York to New Delhi via Dubai. I listened to my favourite
songs, drank multiple glasses of scotch, and read, re-read and
re-re-read everything that was written to me. I read so much
that by the time my plane was about to land in New Delhi,
I obnoxiously felt that I was the messiah coming over to
'transform' Indian football.

Well, my bags did not arrive, nor did the driver Dentsu had
set up, so I spent the next hour in the airport using very broken
Hindi to borrow random people's phones so that I could figure
out my next step. I lost my cool a few times and would not be
lying when I say that the thought of just walking over to the
departures area and buying a ticket back home did not cross my

mind. It was during that chaos that I thought to myself, *How am I going to make any difference in this country if I can't even get out of the airport without freaking out*? This scene perfectly encapsulates my time living in India—an endless succession of lofty dreams, jarring reality, deep introspection and expansive personal and professional growth.

Yes, I did it! I followed my formula and made a move to India. And, over fourteen years after that dramatic landing in New Delhi, I am still in the country. As I relive my transition from NYC to this beautiful country, there are a few key learnings that I would like to highlight regarding this transition period of my life:

## Make a Calculated Choice

While my move to India in 2009 may have seemed like an impulsive decision to most, it was a calculated choice set in motion three years earlier during my first trip to the country in 2006.

## Self-reflect

The ten action points that I came up with in early 2007 were a turning point for my India story. I could have easily returned from my first trip, gone back to work and waited until the confused energy dissipated. Instead, I took time for self-reflection, and journalled, not knowing where it would all lead. It was the momentum created by taking these actions that opened up a new reality for me.

## Research, Research and Research

I needed to research the results of my formula before taking the giant leap. When it became clear that I wanted to work with football in India in some capacity, I researched this topic through every medium available: online articles, regular industry conversations and even a two-and-a-half-week fact-finding trip to better understand the landscape. There was a point in 2009 that I felt like I knew more about football in India than most people living in India, just as a result of the amount of research I had done.

## Act on Your Mission Statement

It was my mission statement that allowed me to stand tall and stay strong through every question thrown my way about my choice to leave MLS and move to India. It became my best friend and trusted ally at the time. I cannot stress enough the importance of getting grounded in your narrative. Also, having the confidence to share it over and over again so that those around you either accept it or stop discussing it with you. Remember, you will not convince everyone about why you want to follow your formula, so do not waste your time trying.

## It Is Okay to Be Afraid And Act Anyway

The giant leaps in life are not meant to be easy. You will get butterflies in your stomach, middle-of-the-night sweats and disempowering thoughts. That is the beauty of the process. If you believe in yourself and what you are choosing to do in the world, this force will carry you forward. Take action despite the fear to maintain the momentum. This means having that tough conversation, sending that honest email, writing that resignation letter and taking that research trip to an unknown place.

'Most people are searching for a path to success that is both easy and certain. Most paths are neither.' — Seth Godin

# 11

# Potential Pitfalls Become a
# Thing of the Past

*But What If You Are Still Not Convinced?*

I have been speaking to people about how to create their
dream jobs for nearly two decades now and what is incredible
is that no matter where I am the same 'But … What about
…?' questions will come up. These are not questions to me
though. I view them as potential pitfalls because the mind
is always going to choose the most risk-averse path. The
mind is afraid of the unknown and will throw up as many
red flags as possible to convince the self that it is best to take
the road most travelled instead of paving a path towards self-
fulfilment.

I would like to address some of these questions I have
often been asked and that may arise in your mind regarding the
process of building your dream career.

### 'How Do I Make Money?'

It is not logical to think that you must only pursue a 'guaranteed' high-salaried career to make enough money to live a quality standard of life. Here is why:

When I was growing up, having a 'good career' meant that you must be a doctor, engineer or lawyer. I am someone who shuts his eyes at the sight of blood, can barely screw a bottle cap back on a bottle and gets lost in legal jargon. So, I knew that I would be terrible if I pursued a career in any of these three professions, which is precisely why *I did not*.

If you think about it, there are people who have had successful careers in every type of profession you can imagine: jugglers, magicians, artists, photographers, restaurant reviewers; heck, there are even sleep consultants who get paid to sleep on hotel beds and share their experience. Even at a young age, I knew that if I worked in an area of life that I excelled at and enjoyed, money would follow me because I would be good at my job. It is logical. *Companies and people pay individuals who do a good job and get results.*

I secured my first full-time professional job in sports when I was twenty-three years old, and over the past two decades, I have always had enough money to pay back my student loan and live a quality life. During this time, some of my dear friends who were investment bankers lost their jobs and wealth during the 2008 financial meltdown. Friends who have been doctors got burnt out from the rigorous schedule and mental exhaustion and took a few years off with no salary in order to recover. And there are friends who have been laid off from top engineering firms due to automation and outsourcing.

At the same time, I have many friends in these professions, earning what most would consider a high income. What I am trying to share is that there is no guarantee that pursuing a career in a high-paying industry is going to earn you a sustained higher-than-average salary. Given this, would it not make sense to pursue a career in an area of life that you are naturally inclined to be good at and actually enjoy?

It is quite simple, usually people who are good at their job and enjoy what they are doing achieve consistent positive results. This can lead to recognition, promotions and increased opportunities in and outside of their organization, all avenues towards earning a higher salary.

### 'How Do I Know For Sure That My Passion, And/Or Superpower And/Or Purpose Are Correct?'

This question typically arises from a fearful, insecure mind which questions whether you are really capable and, to some extent *worthy*, of pursuing a dream career.

The easy answer here is to just keep working on your process. Your initial answers during the process, especially the first time you do this work, form your hypothesis. And like a scientist, you must test your hypothesis in all sorts of situations, evaluate the results and either keep going or course-correct if required. Be more creative and adventurous and test them out via personal projects, family programmes, community events, volunteering, internships or through a part-time job.

As you start engaging in activities around your formula, start to gauge the results of your efforts and how you feel during and after the activity. When I was creating the community football camp for Hyundai, it was clear that I was not only good at it, but I also never felt exhausted while working on the project. This would have been the same if I were organizing a football tournament for my family in my backyard or standing in front of a thousand kids in India, discussing how football has made a difference in my life.

Paras spent his weekends after his event planning course volunteering at events to practise what he learned, gain relevant experience and ensure that this was the professional path he would like to pursue. And Avantika chose to offer her services as an expressive arts therapist in hospitals and schools before making this her full-time career.

*Do the work.* Be creative and come up with different ways to test out your hypothesis and see what results surface. Do not worry if you fail. Just keep being honest with yourself around the results and how you 'feel', as this is the best indicator of whether or not you are truly in line with your formula. And when it comes to the results, do not expect to be extraordinary at the first go. Just like most practices, the more you engage with the activity, the better you will get.

## 'What if I Come Up With Too Many Passions, Superpowers and Purposes?'

The funny thing is that this question is typically asked as a way to say, 'Since I do not know which answers to choose to build my formula, I will continue down a path which is not fully aligned with my natural self.' It is also incredible when I hear this spoken about as a problem instead of an opportunity. You are one of the blessed individuals who has the ability to create multiple formulae and pursue multiple paths. I was stuck with only one path at the time, as I could not come up with more passions, superpowers and purposes; however, I would have been happy to have more options to play with.

My honest answer is to get a whiteboard and create multiple *formulae* working with your various interests, strengths and purposes. Also, feel free to combine them into one formula. For example, I have a good friend who loves both music and football, and it is no surprise that he was able to create a career producing anthems for football clubs around the world. I have another friend who loves wine, poetry and creating environments where people can express themselves without judgement and ended up establishing a highly successful spoken-word poetry wine bar in New York.

There is a possibility that you are someone who embodies 'multipotentiality'. This is an educational and psychological term referring to the ability and preference of a person, particularly one of strong intellectual or artistic curiosity, to excel in two or more different fields. If you fit into this category, the bad news is that you may feel some pressure or confusion during the early stages of the process because your mind, body and spirit will protest the idea of coming up with just a few career paths to traverse.

The good news is that people with multipotentialities are blessed with the ability to learn rapidly, synthesize ideas and be adaptable, which means that you will most likely find success in any area that lights you up. So, if you are a specialist like me or a multipotentialite like many of my close friends, take on the process work as all roads on this path lead to the same place: professional fulfilment.

The challenge is that most of us have grown up in a left-brained world where we are taught that there are existing boxes, and we must pick the one we think fits us the best or are told by others which one we should choose. The best thing we can do is expand or modify the box to be slightly more comfortable within the one we picked. Creativity is an art, not a science, so you must tap into your right brain to design a new box instead of feeling limited to the ones presented to you.

Once you get into the box, you can immediately break down its walls and have endless space to play.

## 'How Do I Convince My Reluctant Family to Accept My Non-traditional Career Pathway?'

There is this widely used and completely limiting phrase commonly said in many North Indian households, *'log kya kahenge'* which essentially means what will people say? It is usually accompanied by wide eyes and a disapproving click of the tongue when young ones make non- traditional choices. It is typically used by concerned family members (and the immediate social circle) to ensure that you dress in a certain way; marry a particular type of person; attend all essential family functions; have children at the 'right' age and engage in professional work accepted by the community. I experienced it at home and various Indian community events. The unsaid statement around careers was, 'Do what brings you money and *sounds good* when we tell our family and friends.'

And it is not just Indians. Something similar to 'log kya kahenge' would show up in households in every country around the world, of course, some more extreme than others. I used to get angry, annoyed and frustrated when anyone in my family or community even innocently questioned my choice to pursue a 'non-traditional' career pathway. But as I matured, I saw their concern from a different perspective: ultimately your support system, the people who love you, just want you to be financially secure so that you are happy. It may come up in the form of preachy uncles and gossipy aunties, but underneath it, there is a harmless intention. Once I understood this, I stopped fighting it and I channelized my energy into creating happiness through my work, knowing that professional fulfilment would make me happy, making the people who love me happy as well.

Just assume that there will be resistance with you choosing your formula to guide your career creation as opposed to taking the roads accepted by your community. The mind is trained to be risk-averse, and that is no different from the minds of those who love and care for you. As soon as you begin to head down a path that they are unsure of, an objection will be raised, and they will feel like it is their duty to guide you back onto a safer road.

The key is to remain committed and compassionate—committed to achieving ongoing fulfilment through creating your dream job(s) and compassionate for those around you who are not aligned with your choices. Listen to them, do not fight back and always remember that they are coming from a place of love. But do not, not even for a single second, stop taking steps in the direction of your career fulfilment.

100,000 hours is a lot of hours, and do not waste them to keep your parents happy or quiet down the gossip mongers that exist in all our communities. *It is your life*, and your happiness will serve existence in the most beautiful way. Never feel selfish for choosing yourself when it comes to building your career. And, trust me, if you do the process work and take the aligned actions, you will be on your way to securing your dream job, kick-starting your dream career and experiencing professional joy, thus fulfilling the underlying intention of everyone who loves you.

### How Do I Make a Career Switch?

I am a firm believer that no amount of money can justify not enjoying your professional life, especially if you have invested so much time, money, blood, sweat and tears into your education. That said, I am aware that many people end up getting into a job that may not be aligned with their formula. Then money starts coming in and then promotions and then mortgage payments and then kids and then school fees and then one day they wake up and feel trapped professionally. They are resigned, telling themselves something along the lines of 'I work to live, I don't live to work' in order to justify showing up each day to a place that they do not like, to do work that does not fulfil them.

'Choose a job you love and you will never have to work a day in your life.' — Confucius

I neither live to work nor work to live. I choose to enjoy my life, all of it, not just the hours when I am not in my office. Most people are not aware of the type of negative energy they bring into their homes when they feel trapped, frustrated and beaten down by the everyday rigours of an unfulfilling career. It is sad because I have been around amazing parents who work tirelessly to give their children the best of everything. But they are unable to spend quality time with their kids due to never-ending work responsibilities. Many need to numb themselves through mindless television or substances upon coming home from work to disconnect from the previous eight or more hours of survival.

I am not generalizing; my experience has been that the situation described above is the norm, not the exception. We just have very powerful and sneaky minds that can justify anything to absolve ourselves from the responsibility of making a drastic change to our lives in order to thrive. This can be seen with individuals who have endured an energy-sucking or toxic relationship for an extended period. The fear aligned with change is so intense that we would rather remain in the situation and endure the pain day after day than walk away and enter unknown terrain.

This is not living life; this is living in wartime circumstances. It is survival, which is the worst way to choose to live life. I get that running a household, taking care of a family and other commitments can be challenging, and my advice is not to put the book down and draft a resignation email to your boss right now. Not at all; my recommendation is that you pause, take a few deep breaths and imagine a version of yourself where your professional scope of work completely fulfils you. That you respect your organization, your colleagues and, most importantly, feel stimulated, engaged and enthusiastic about the privilege of serving through your professional responsibilities. That you wake up each day pumped up to start your work and complete the day bursting with feelings of connection, joy and accomplishment that you bring into your home and pour all over your loved ones.

Spend minutes, hours, days, doing this daily. Start from scratch, do not get caught up with logic or logistics, come from a place of emptiness, as if anything is possible. Feel free to discuss your passions, superpowers and purposes with your loved ones, make the process fun but do not let it get influenced by others; always differentiate between what *feels right* versus what *sounds right*. Start identifying the different career opportunities. See if there are opportunities in your current organization and, if not, explore creating a 'side hustle' that is in line with your formula. If required, sign up for short- or long-term courses that can help you build relevant knowledge and experience in the subject matter aligned with your formula.

Let the space of possibility and momentum brought about by focused S-M-A-R-T steps create new worlds for you. You will be amazed at the results manifested by all the positive progress and increased energy you feel during the process.

I want to quickly touch on a sensitive, but important point around money. During the process, it is critical to ask yourself, 'How much money do I really need?' Sometimes we get caught up on a conveyor belt where we make money, spend money and dream of bigger things, so we try to make more money to get those things, and then the belt just keeps moving forward.

'Some people are so poor, all they have is money.'
— Bob Marley

As humans, we often live in a mindset of scarcity even though, in reality, we have abundance within and around us. It is essential to sit with yourself and possibly the appropriate decision-makers in your family. See how much is required to live the quality of life that would fulfil your family's needs and many of your desires as well. I have found that this exercise creates clarity and typically removes or significantly reduces the fear around making a career decision that could impact the amount of income you may earn. It also makes your loved ones feel like a part of the process instead of the victims of a seemingly impulsive and selfish decision, which can create negative emotions and affect your journey towards your dream job.

'All of life is a foreign country.' — Jack Kerouac

# 12

# Learn the Rules of the
# Game to Play It Well

*How Do You Remain on Your Dream Career Path?*

Have you ever worked out for several weeks straight, felt good and promised yourself that you will always make time for exercise? Only to give up a few days later and justify it to yourself with a million excuses. Checking in, applying the formula, crafting the mission statement and taking the S-M-A-R-T steps will open up multiple opportunities for you to create a fulfilling career(s) throughout your lifetime. But people have the tendency to continue with their default thoughts and patterns.

It is illogical that we would actively choose not to do something that we know makes us feel better and live longer, but humans are funny creatures. This aspect of human behaviour has been around for hundreds of years, and I cannot claim that I fix, change or transform it immediately. All I can do is share some rules that will help you stay on the path of heart versus head, purpose versus practicality and the unknown versus known.

## Rule #1 Understand the Role of Your Soul, Spirit and Emotions

Soul, spirit and emotions can impact our lives. Feel free to replace 'soul' and 'spirit' with any words that feel more comfortable.

Written into your soul is your mission, your purpose in this lifetime or how you want to contribute to the world. This is what provides you with genuine and lasting fulfilment and allows you to move forward even during the darkest of hours.

Your spirit is the energy that fuels your efforts, enthusiasm and curiosity around your soul's mission. This is what allows someone to work for hours on a project without getting tired. Or continue researching a particular topic just out of pure curiosity regardless of whether or not it leads to job advancement. Or wake up excited to go to work for no reason at all.

Finally, there are emotions that are temporary and can either positively or negatively impact the intensity of your spirit. If things are going your way and you are happy with others, and yourself, the chances are that your spirit will be high. If things are falling apart and you are disappointed or disconnected from the people around you, the chances are that your spirit will be low. The key is to be aware of this chain reaction.

This knowledge has come from a mind-opening conversation with my friend and spiritual teacher, Naveen Varshneya, who runs a leading research and treatment centre called NV Life and has authored a transformational book called *Meditation —The Cure*.

In a broad sense, my soul had me leave my life behind in the United States in 2009 to move to India to serve as a catalyst for the creation of a thriving football ecosystem in this country. And it has been my spirit that has kept me fully involved, engaged and enthused in this mission for well over a decade. Despite all this, my emotions can quickly work against me to decrease the spirit in which I pursue my mission. Because like all humans, I have bad moments, bad days and even bad weeks, but I always make sure that these times do not significantly impact the power of my spirit for too long or make me question what is written on my soul.

Let me share an experience. When I was the CEO of a professional football club in India, our senior team was playing its final group stage match in the Federation Cup against Shillong Lajong. A draw or win would pretty much assure us of a place in the semi-finals. The score was 2–2, Shillong was down to ten men due to an earlier red card, we were pressing for the win and then in injury time, we let up a goal due to a silly mistake. It was heartbreaking, especially since this was probably the eighth time over the past year that we let up a goal in the dying minutes of a match to lose points. Our season was over.

Immediately after the match ended, a major windstorm hit Pune, and our entire operations set-up for the next day's open trials for our academy was destroyed. Not only did this mean that we would lose money to replace the equipment, it meant that most of my staff would have to stay up all night, setting everything up again. At that moment, I can comfortably say that my spirit was very low. I was angry at football, my club, myself, the weather, everyone. I just wanted to cancel the trials and the planned Grassroots Festival and spend that weekend sulking at home. But 'the show must go on', and we all pulled together to ensure we were prepared for the next forty-eight hours of football programming taking place at the campus. Even though I was in action, my spirit remained low all through the night.

After only a few hours of sleep, which were mostly filled with replays in my mind of Shillong's third goal, I managed to get out of bed at 4:30 a.m., head over to the football facility and lead our 6:15 a.m. operations meeting. Still, in my sulking state, I communicated to the staff to open the security gates and let the trialists in for the 7:00 a.m. registration. What I witnessed next blew me away: *600 players were eagerly trotting towards the registration desk with their boots in their hands and dreams of some day playing for our academy in their hearts.* The next twelve hours were a blur of interactions with hundreds of parents hungry to have their sons join the programme. This included conversations with our coaches about talented players and presentations about life at our academy. Neither the three hours of sleep nor the blistering heat slowed me down. Even by the end of the day, I returned home feeling high on life.

I woke up early the next day, excited to get back to the campus and interact with my staff, the trialists and their parents. Negative thoughts of the loss to Shillong Lajong or lack of sleep no longer troubled me. The day went by successfully. The cherry on top was an extraordinary Grassroots Festival organized by our coaches for a group of underprivileged youth, orphans and individuals with physical disabilities who came to us through a Pune-based non-profit organization.

I smiled for the entire three hours of the festival. Just a ball, some committed coaches and a group of enthusiastic and inspiring children created a magical environment full of love, laughter, play and togetherness. Its power impacted everyone involved in the event—the whole pitch was just one big smile. Thankfully, I had invited Avantika, to join in the festivities as a volunteer, as there was no way that I could have adequately recreated this magical experience for her.

When I finally got home late Sunday night, I felt drunk, babbling about how incredible the trials and the Grassroots Festival were and how blessed I felt to be involved with this sport. I realized—thanks to the positive response, interactions and experiences over the weekend—that my spirit took a 180-degree turn. I could not wait to get to work the next day, and I was already planning personal trips to the non-profit organization for Avantika and me so that we could facilitate football and art workshops for the children. I was thinking about ways to ensure we make such grassroots festivals a regular part of our club's programming next year and exploring partnerships to expand our trials into new territories. Even now, as I write this, my heart starts to smile, reflecting upon the incredible experiences I had interacting with over a thousand footballers from across India, as well as all those that participated in the festival.

So, it is inevitable (unless you are enlightened) that circumstances will affect your emotions, impacting your spirit. The key is not to run away from your soul's mission, no matter how severe the impact. As just around the corner is a weekend full of activities and interactions which will surely excite and inspire you, raise your spirit and realign yourself with the enthusiasm and curiosity surrounding your soul's purpose in this lifetime.

'Remember that sometimes not getting what you want is a wonderful stroke of luck.' — Dalai Lama

## Rule #2 Make Sure You are Flowing in the Right Direction

Have you ever watched a flowing stream? Not every section of the stream is peaceful and smooth. There are all sorts of obstacles impeding the water. However, no matter what comes in its way, the stream just keeps flowing in its natural direction. Your career pathway is no different. You are flowing down a stream for 100,000 hours, and it is up to you to ensure that you are flowing in the right direction.

There was a point in 2008 when I looked up my stream at MLS and saw the director of marketing position. If I were honest with myself, while the thought of being the director of marketing of MLS would be a dream come true for millions of people, it was not my dream any more. The position primarily focused on brand building, market research and increasing the league's television viewership. While these are all critical business requirements of any professional sports league, they were not completely aligned with my formula, which, at the time, was creating programmes and partnerships to grow the Indian football landscape. And since MLS was not seriously considering expanding into Asia back then, it was clear that my stream was no longer flowing in the right direction.

When I thought of my next job after MLS, I always felt that it would be with the Fédération Internationale de Football Association (FIFA), the Asian Football Confederation (AFC) or the All India Football Federation. Never in a hundred years did I imagine that it would be in the sports division of a Japanese advertising agency based in New Delhi. However, my stream wanted to flow into the direction of Indian football. I understood that Dentsu would give me the required exposure to Indian business, media and entertainment, in addition to sports, which would ultimately help me become a more effective Indian sports management professional.

While Dentsu was not my dream organization, and my role was not a position that I saw myself staying in for many years, I knew that I was flowing in the right direction there. Because, I was able to work on the largest Indian sports events at the time. This included experiences with the Indian Premier League (IPL), the 2010 Commonwealth Games, the Indian Grand Prix Formula 1, I-League and the Professional Golf Tour of India (PGTI), in addition to interacting with most of the companies investing in Indian sports and travelling to all corners of the country to better understand the landscape.

So, every once in a while, stop and look upstream and ensure that you are flowing in the right direction. If you are not, then do the process work to course correct. Do not worry if your first job on the new path is not everything you envisioned; just ensure that it includes all three magical elements and is flowing towards the direction of your dream career.

## Rule #3 Invest in Yourself

We have countless beliefs, emotions and attachments around money that we must address to further our growth, but, at the very least, learn to differentiate investment from luxury. All relationships require some investment—investment of time, love, friendship, energy, etc. *Your relationship with your formula is a relationship that requires life-long investment.* This means understanding what will help you strengthen your formula, causing an expansion of self and being comfortable with making those investments.

The high that comes with nurturing your formula is natural and, typically, a sustained high. Spending on a luxury item or experience is something entirely different. A luxury item or experience typically comes with an expiration date, while an investment can reap benefits over a lifetime. Investing in your growth is a genuine investment versus indulgences or pouring money into guilty pleasures.

Over the years, I have chosen to make it a priority to invest more in intangible assets like nurturing my formula, expanding my heart and de-cluttering my mind versus tangible assets. In actual terms, this looks like joining presentation skills classes at local universities, going on multiple heart-centric retreats in the Himalayas or taking up 10-day Vipassana courses. These are just some personal examples, and each of these would require an investment of time, money or energy, or all of the above. I am willing to make those investments, knowing that they will keep me on the path of living a purposeful life. The meditation courses provided me with the knowledge and tools that I needed to remain grounded and calm during my tumultuous first year in India. This included letting go of a difficult relationship and spending a month in a hospital as a result of a series of unfortunate events caused by an infection in my stomach.

This does not mean that I do not go on non-growth-focused trips, buy materials like electronics, clothes or furniture or spend time chilling out with friends. It simply means that my priority will always go into the investment that will nurture my formula, and I will not feel guilty of expenditure in this direction. I can spend any amount of money on courses, retreats, festivals and research trips and feel peace in my heart, knowing that the money is going to a good place. This highlights the need to keep checking in and being honest with your authentic self, as only you will know what for you would be considered an investment versus a luxury. With this honesty, you will prioritize your budget and let go of unnecessary feelings of guilt when it comes to spending on something that you know will help you live a more fulfilled life.

## Rule #4 Support Others on Their Career Pathway

One of the challenges with successfully identifying and living a life aligned with your formula is that the path you are paving is typically a unique one, so, at times, it can be difficult to see where others fit in. This has the possibility of causing isolation, arrogance and moving forward at a rapid pace without stopping to collaborate with or check in on those around you. You must understand the impact people have on your life and how important it is to support others on their career path.

'We rise by lifting others.' — Robert G. Ingersoll

My professional success has been the result of following my formula, taking the support of others, and empowering those around me to identify and work towards their dream jobs. I have been on teams where everyone is just working for a salary, and I have also been on teams where each person is living their dream, and we have all been working together towards a larger collective vision. I can stake my life on the fact that the latter situation will always be more fruitful and fulfilling, especially during some of the more challenging times. It is the alignment towards our individual and collective missions and visions that carries us forward when the road gets rocky.

Hence, when you come across someone with a similar formula see it as a blessing. It is an opportunity to learn from one another and possibly collaborate if the situation calls for it.

Over the past two decades, while working in the sports and education industries, I have made it my practice to actively seek out others who have a similar formula as I do and explore ways to collaborate. This is how I have met and pioneered new paths with extraordinary people like Sukhvinder Singh who is one of the most passionate and enterprising individuals in the Indian sports industry, Gaurav Modwel who is one of the most intelligent and energetic individuals in the Indian sports industry, and Joy Bhattacharjya who is one of the most creative and respected people in the Indian sports industry and the project director of the highly successful 2017 FIFA U-17 World Cup. Also, I have made it a point to acknowledge who is clearly on their path and ask the self-reflection questions to those still trying to figure out where they are going. This practice has helped me build an incredible network of relationships with people all over the world who are—in some way, shape, or form—supporting my dream professional life.

## Rule #5 Share Your Mission Statement with the World

There are many cultural differences that I have experienced when interacting with people in the United States, compared to in India. One of them has to do with self-expression. Now I may be generalizing, but I think that Americans are more comfortable expressing themselves, even if they do not have everything figured out. While most people in India are fine with talking about history, concepts, ideas, or other people, but when it comes to expressing their authentic selves—who they are and what they are up to in the world—they can hold back. This would be completely fine in some contexts and environments, but given the fact that people have a role to play in opening up doors along your dream jobs path, this does not always work.

Once you are clear with your mission statement, use every possible medium to express it in the world. We are inherently attracted to authentic people and want to be around and support them. There is just something about truth spoken confidently that is sexy, and we are magnetized by it. So, when you authentically express your mission statement, people will come out of the woodwork to help you along to create new realities that did not exist before within your lens.

Make your mission statement your brand. This can be done through traditional media, social media—which is the most cost-effective medium available to reach the masses—community groups, individual conversations, volunteering, etc. The key is just to let your mission statement show up as who you are in the world and watch the world deliver the unthinkable through its citizens. And not everyone will immediately react in the way that you want. But know that inner truth when expressed powerfully will always be respected and will ensure that seeds are being planted within the fabric of the universe.

Through the expression of my mission statement, I was blessed with people like Mark Noonan, Geoff Hayes, Dianne Lynch, David Wright, Sunil Gulati, Tarun Chaudhry, Sukhvinder Singh, Shirish Kulkarni, Vivek Sethia and Gaurav Modwel. They opened up new doors for me to always live a professional life that was a natural extension of myself. And beyond them, it has been thanks to regular expression of who I am and what I am up to in the world that I have been able to get opportunities to travel across India and all over the world, speaking at conferences, delivering guest lectures and consulting various sports organizations. As I said before, people are inherently attracted to truth, and the more authentic you are with your mission statement, the more doors will open, and opportunities will come your way.

'To be yourself in a world that is constantly trying to make you something else is the greatest accomplishment.'
— Ralph Waldo Emerson

# 13

# Professional Fulfilment Matters

*What Is Really Important in Your Career?*

## How I Chose to be Happy

Projects and people create more happiness and fulfilment in our lives than designations and pay package. I will stand by this statement until the day I die because I have lived this over the past twenty years while working professionally across multiple continents. But then you may wonder: Who does not want to be a CEO with a handsome salary? It is fine, as long as you are enthusiastic about the projects you are working on and are aligned with the people you are working with.

It is human nature to want to be happy. And just like luxuries, job profile and earned income have a limit on the level and duration of happiness they can offer someone. Eventually, the joy derived from these two will run out. Unfulfilling projects and people you do not resonate with will accelerate this depletion. If this was not the case, there should be no turnover at any successful and high-profile company, but there is. *Why?*

Because employees get burned out or no longer align with the projects, people or values of the company. Eventually, the money that someone is making and the power they feel they hold with their designation and company name listed on their business card or LinkedIn profile cannot justify the frustration or hollowness they may feel inside. But there is good news. *There is always good news.*

You can make career choices focused on engaging projects and like-minded people versus any other available criteria.

It was 2011. I had been living in India for nearly two years, and the media reported that International Management Group (IMG) and Reliance Industries Limited (RIL) were entering into a joint venture in India. They would be purchasing the marketing rights for football and basketball for the next fifteen and thirty years, respectively. At the time, IMG was the top sports management company in the world and Reliance was (and still is) one of India's largest conglomerates—a match seemingly made in heaven. My friends at the AIFF confirmed that the new agency, called IMG-R, would be the biggest sports management company in India and primarily focus on the development of football in the country.

This was the break I had been waiting for since leaving MLS. I was missing being part of an entity that sits at the top of the football pyramid, as this typically offers more of an opportunity to make a national impact, which was my intention at the time. Thanks to a few contacts at IMG in New York and London, I was able to set up a meeting with the managing director of the new joint venture. I flew from New Delhi to Mumbai, headed to the IMG-R office located along the Western Expressway in Bandra East, and sat down with the MD for a conversation. We spoke for an hour. During that time, I realized that while on paper working for IMG-R would have been a dream, it may take years for these two large organizations to comfortably merge their assets and strengths and figure out how they would want to grow football in India.

On the other side, Sukhvinder, my friend from the AIFF, had recently been appointed MD of a US-headquartered football agency called Libero Sports that had opened up an office in New Delhi. From the day I arrived in India in October 2009, Sukhvinder had quickly grown from an acquaintance to my closest friend, an Indian football industry guide and confidant. He mentioned that he was putting together a team of three to four people to build up the agency and that he would like me to come on board as a director and head up the consultancy division. Initially, I wrote it off. *How could I go from working with one of the world's leading advertising agencies to join a small firm?* It was a challenging idea for me to accept, made harder every time I thought of myself sitting at the top of the Indian football pyramid with IMG-R.

However, after my realization that IMG-R may take time to establish itself, I was torn. Even more so when a few days after the meeting, I received a call from IMG-R offering me a position in their football division and a salary which was much higher than what I was earning at Dentsu. I spent a week deliberating on all the pros and cons of the opportunity. During that time, Sukhvinder had rounded out his core team made up of young, passionate, intelligent and hard-working individuals and introduced me to the company's American investors. They had good values and were looking at India from a strategic and long-term perspective. A day before my deadline to share a decision with IMG-R, I headed down to Lodhi Gardens in Central New Delhi, sat on my favourite bench, and wrote out the pros and cons of each organization as it related to my career.

| LIBERO SPORTS | | IMG-R | |
|---|---|---|---|
| PROs | CONs | PROs | CONs |
| Like-minded owners & team | New company that is a minnow in the sports industry | Top sports management agency in India | Will take a while until football development strategy is clear |
| I can design my role as I please | Salary is competitive but not as high as my perceived value | Salary offered is reflective of my perceived value | Not clear about who is in power, IMG or RIL, could be an issue |
| Long-term vision to professionalize the Indian football ecosystem at all levels | Office is in a business centre in a nondescript building in Gurugram | Office is located in a nice building in the heart of Mumbai | The initial focus is more on establishing a league *vs* grassroots development |
| Fully passionate about Indian football | No high-profile clients or projects as yet | Part of a global network of agencies | Seems like a hierarchical structure |

By the end of the exercise, I was clear. I must go with the organization where I know I would experience joy regardless of the company's profile or the salary offered. I immediately called up Sukhvinder and accepted the offer to join Libero Sports.

*Any regrets*?
None!

## Projects and People *or* Profile and Pay?

This ended up being the best decision I could have possibly made. Over five years at Libero Sports, we built the top football consulting firm in the country. We became the go-to group for anyone interested in either investing or enhancing their investment in Indian football. This allowed me to work with the world's top clubs, establish relationships with nearly every Indian football stakeholder, spend time with the Indian government and advise large companies interested in investing in the beautiful game.

Beyond the extensive knowledge I gained while working with Sukhvinder and travelling around the country studying Indian football, the best part was the family bond we had with our team at Libero Sports. From the owners to my colleagues, we all respected one another and worked hard as a team to achieve our mission of pioneering the growth of the Indian football industry.

On the other side, a few of my friends who had taken up positions with IMG-R left within a year due to the challenges bound to arise during the early stages of a joint venture. It was not until 2014, three years after I took up the position with Libero Sports, that IMG-R started to make its mark in Indian football with the establishment of the Indian Super League. Now, many years later, I can comfortably say that IMG-R, currently operating as Reliance Sports, is one of the leaders in sports management and development in India and a place that anyone would aspire to work.

*So, projects and people generate more happiness and fulfilment than profile and pay.* After leaving Libero Sports in 2016, I became the CEO of a professional football club and the Liverpool FC International Academy—DSK Shivajians, Pune, a landmark youth development project that I had helped establish while at Libero Sports. As a CEO, my salary increased by three times more, but I can honestly say that I derived more happiness during my time at Libero Sports. While it would be a dream of most football enthusiasts to run a professional football club and world-class academy, I can comfortably say that this position was *not* a natural extension of myself, at least not in 2016.

While serving as CEO of DSK Shivajians FC, I no longer had the opportunity to build sustainable partnerships and programmes to further the Indian football ecosystem. Most of my time was spent troubleshooting governance and administrative challenges in the Indian professional football landscape besides dealing with several internal issues caused by employees who struggled to work together, and helping our foreign technical staff settle down in Pune. When I looked upstream, I could not quite tell when my time working through my 100,000 hours would go back to being aligned with my formula. I would come home unhappy most days and kept justifying it to myself by saying things like, 'This is the best job in Indian football, so just be happy' or 'You just got married, and the pay is great, so keep on doing this job for your family'.

In addition to running the football club, I was also serving as a visiting faculty at a Pune-based university, teaching marketing strategy, sports marketing and the business of football to MBA students. On top of teaching the classes, I had to put together the academic curriculum from scratch, grade papers and provide mentorship for students. I also had to drive three hours round trip to and from my home in Mundwa to the university campus in Lavale. It was my first time teaching full courses, as up until then, I was a serial guest lecturer, which was to me more of a 'fun uncle' role versus the course lecturer who played the role of a 'committed parent'.

Many of my lectures took place on weekends. I remember that, on those days, I would wake up at 5:30 a.m., spend about an hour and a half exercising and meditating, and then practise my lecture in the mirror for about two hours before heading over to the campus in a taxi. I would then teach for eight hours, come home in the evening, grade papers and then begin preparing for my next day of classes. I was making 1,500 rupees an hour, which comes to less than $20 and does not include the many hours spent travelling or grading papers.

Was I insane?

*Hell, no!*

When I was in the educational environment, I just found myself more engaged while working on my course content, delivery and evaluation than I was with most of my responsibilities as the club's chief executive.

Do not get me wrong; I had a wonderful boss, Shirish Kulkarni, the club owner, who created the opportunity for me to build a professional football club model that other investors in India could emulate. And I worked extremely hard to build a strong squad that would be competitive on the field, develop supporters, establish effective internal systems and processes, and create harmony in the office.

I was just simply aligned with the idea of educating and empowering the next generation of global sports leaders and experienced myself as more effective at this than running the club. At that time, my energy was better served being channelized towards education and mentorship of youth hungry for it than firefighting for a professional football team. No matter how much money I received or how much respect and importance I was given as CEO, this feeling simply would not change.

Trust me, I am not someone who has so much money that I can comfortably leave a high-paying, less satisfying role for one that it is low-paying, but highly fulfilling. My parents come from humble backgrounds and, although they had provided a superb quality of life for Paras and me, they tried their best to teach us how to save, and we did not listen. From my first professional job at MLS in 2003 to when I got married in 2016, I never really saved money. I lived in carefree abundance, assuming that money would always find me, and somehow I have always had enough to live my version of a good life.

After our wedding, Avantika sat me down and wrote out our savings strategy, which I have dutifully followed ever since. Though, just a year after our marriage and with limited savings, I was profoundly contemplating my future as CEO without clarity of how things would work out financially. Regardless, I was still open to choosing the happiness that comes with professional fulfilment versus the contentment resulting from a prestigious-sounding designation and a high monthly salary. This openness created the space for the birth of the most impactful and fulfilling project of my career.

'Pleasure in the job puts perfection in the work.'
— Aristotle

# 14

# The Steps I Took to Design
# My Dream Career

*How the Process Can Help You Enjoy a Fulfilling Career?*

## Checking in

Whenever I feel a misalignment between my inner and outer selves I reconnect with the process. When I started to understand that the internal signs around my CEO position were not just a phase, I packed my bag, drove for two hours to Panchgani and ended up checking into a simple, peaceful cottage on a cliff overlooking a canyon with a ravine below. I settled in, went over to the balcony, opened my notebook and started answering the self-reflection questions. What I discovered was my new formula:

[(Passion: Self-development) + (Superpower: Get people interested in or excited about something that has touched, moved or inspired me)] x Purpose: Empowering the next generation of global sports leaders =

- Aligned Jobs (Passion + Superpower)
  - Teacher
  - Motivational speaker
  - Life coach
- Possible Dream Jobs (when purpose is included)
  - Sports management lecturer
  - Career counsellor for aspiring sports managers
  - Sports management education programme director

For the first time since I could remember, my passion was not football, and even my purpose had slightly shifted. However, the essence of how I wanted to contribute to the world was still similar. I had always seen myself as someone working at the highest levels of football. However, my authentic self was saying that self-development and education were more aligned with who I was then and what I would like to manifest in the world than pure sport. I must admit that this new realization was daunting, and at first, I did not know what to do with it.

'I have no special talents. I am only passionately curious.'
— Albert Einstein

It should not have come as a surprise, though. Since 2007, I had been actively engaged in leadership and self-expression programmes through Landmark Education, first in NYC, and then in New Delhi, where I took on the role of a coach during multiple programmes. In 2011, I experienced my first spiritual retreat at an Osho ashram in the Himalayas and, since then, had been regularly attending both spiritual and self-development weekend workshops and retreats. Each one having a profound positive impact on my holistic well-being. And every time I completed a programme, I would spend hours exploring how

I could bring these highly effective practices into the sports world. A thought that would be quickly forgotten as soon as I stepped back into my office and immersed myself into my day-to-day work.

## Getting into a Mission Mode

So, I quickly wrote down a few steps that would help me integrate education and self-development into my professional life:

1. Share what is going through my heart with Avantika.
2. Continue teaching courses at the Symbiosis School of Sports Sciences.
3. Offer to teach courses at other sports management institutes in India.
4. Research the global and domestic sports management education landscape.
5. Schedule a meeting with Shirish Kulkarni and share my intent to integrate education and self-development into my role as CEO.
6. Schedule a lunch with the CEO of DSK International Institute of Design to learn about running a postgraduate education programme.
7. Speak with current and former sports management education students to learn more about their programmes.
8. Set up informational interviews with at least three sports management institute programme directors to learn more about this field.
9. Research education-focused conferences that I can attend to build my knowledge and network.

10. Identify organizations that are focused on bringing self-development tools into the sports industry.

I did not want to leave my position with DSK Group. Shirish had been a friend and support from our first meeting in 2013, and I had committed to serving his group, a promise that I had no intention to break. My strategy was to create an opportunity to restructure my role so that I could focus on those areas where I would achieve the best and most fulfilling results for my organization.

I left Panchgani with a plan that I put into action the following day. I shared my feelings with Avantika over breakfast. I decided to write to the director of the Symbiosis School of Sports Sciences, and communicate that I would like to teach more classes to their MBA students. Then I scheduled time with Shirish and shared the initial research I had conducted on the market for sports management education programmes in India and made a case for why DSK Group should explore setting one up. He loved the idea and immediately called Ninad Panse, CEO of the DSK International Institute of Design, and requested that he meet with me the following day to discuss my thoughts around establishing a postgraduate programme in sports management.

Before leaving his office, Shirish and I talked about how we could restructure my CEO role to primarily focus on revenue generation for the club and now, establishing the sports education programme. I would continue to oversee the club from a management perspective.

I could not believe it; within twenty-four hours of returning from my trip to Panchgani, my professional life had completely evolved. I was still overseeing a professional football club *and* establishing a sports management educational institute. The next day Ninad and I had a three-hour meeting where we put our initial thoughts together around an innovative and impactful sports management education programme. That excitement that kicks in when you know that you are creating something special started to emerge during that time.

I went home fully energized and spent every evening that week continuing my research on sports management institutes around the world, speaking with current and former students about their programmes and interacting with institute programme directors to learn the field. Over the next few months, I had countless meetings with Ninad and others in the education space. Finally, I had completed the business plan for a world-class, industry-designed postgraduate sports management programme hosted at the DSK International Campus. The best part was that a large component of the programme entirely focused on the holistic development of the students.

During this time, I also drafted my new mission statement:

*I am deeply committed to educating and empowering the next generation of global sports industry leaders. And given my sixteen years of sports management experience across multiple continents, my extensive self-development work and my time as an educator, I feel that I am perfectly positioned to design and deliver an industry-focused and holistic-learning sports management education programme.*

The whole process of establishing our sports management institute while running a professional football club was invigorating. During this period, I found a whole new source of energy that I had not tapped into for some time, and my relationships inside and outside of the office were far more positive. I was happier and more generous with others and myself. I assumed that Avantika and I would live this life with DSK Group and Pune for many years to come, which excited me since I loved the company and the city.

Then one day, the unexpected happened. Well, as John Lennon once said, 'Life happens when you are busy making other plans.' We heard that DSK Group was facing some severe legal and financial problems due to an issue with one of their large-scale developments called Dream City. At first, it seemed like just a blip on the radar of a successful and respected family-run conglomerate like DSK Group, so none of us at the club were too worried. Then the situation quickly went from bad to worse, and all of a sudden, delayed timelines around the DSK Sports Management Institute were the least of my worries. I had to figure out how to run a club when salaries are no longer getting paid and there was no clarity on the organization's future.

The next few months were the most challenging time in my entire professional life up to that point. I had to tap into everything I have learned from my spiritual and self-development practices to remain grounded and positive. Daily yoga and meditation, affirmations, expressive arts therapy, neuro-linguistic programming, non-violent communication, nature walks—anything that would help me keep my mind clear even though most people associated with the club, including me, had not received a salary for several months. My phone was constantly ringing with messages from people asking for their payments, and the media was slamming our club's management for the situation we were in. And the worst thing was that the financial crisis was completely out of our control, leaving our entire staff feeling powerless.

The saying, 'whatever doesn't kill you, only makes you stronger' was written on the whiteboard in my office, and this proved to be true. During this time, I understood the power of spiritual and self-development practices as when times get tough, which they certainly do in sport, you must engage in activities that give you inner strength, clarity and positive vibes. Those individuals who take this on are the ones that ultimately lead their departments, teams, organizations, or industries out of the darkness. I made best efforts to be that type of leader during this crisis. I promised myself that I would try to help instil these practices in any sports industry professional whom I mentor in the future. It was not easy, and I leaned on many people for support during this time. This was a completely new situation for me to navigate—especially as I was still trying to figure out the country's business and legal systems.

'Do you know a company called India On Track, a leading management and marketing agency?'

While all of this was going on, I received this message from my mentor, former US Soccer president and Columbia University Economics professor, Sunil Gulati. I replied, 'Yes, I have known India On Track for years, and they are doing good work in the training programmes and consultancy space.'

He added that India On Track (IOT) founder and CEO Vivek Sethia had recently visited him at Columbia University and he wanted to get my impressions of the company. I mentioned that I would be seeing Vivek at a football conference in Mumbai in a week and would try to understand what IOT was planning and then share my thoughts with him.

Fast forward one week, and I was in Mumbai attending the Football Movement conference, a high-end international football event organized by IOT. The banquet hall at St. Regis Hotel in Lower Parel was full of some of the biggest personalities in Indian football as well as several senior delegates from the Premier League and Premier League clubs.

During one of the tea breaks, I ran into Vivek and mentioned my exchange with Sunil. Vivek shared that IOT was exploring the idea of establishing something in *sports management education* and would like to have Sunil involved. As soon as I heard the words, 'sports management education' my eyes lit up. I smiled and told Vivek that I would be in touch on this topic and would also let Sunil know that I recommend that he work with IOT on this project.

'Security is mostly a superstition. Life is either a daring adventure or nothing.' — Helen Keller

Later in the evening, I was heading out to dinner with a group from the Premier League, and just as I walked out of the hotel lobby, I saw IOT chairman Gaurav Modwel waiting for his car. I had only met Gaurav once, years before in a meeting at his office when Libero Sports was trying to pitch consultancy services for his Indian Super League club FC Pune City. But I did not know him too well. Something got into me, and I walked straight over to Gaurav.

'Hi, Gaurav, how are you doing?'

'Hi, Neel, I'm doing well. Just about to head home. It's been a long day.'

'Yes, fantastic conference. Congratulations! I had a brief conversation with Vivek earlier today, and he mentioned that India On Track was thinking about starting something in sports management education.'

'Yes, we badly need an industry-designed sports management education course in India.'

(I was getting excited.)

'I completely agree. I've actually been working on a plan for an industry-designed sports management education programme. This is something that I am deeply passionate about and committed to making happen.'

(Gaurav was smiling now.)

'Really? Call me on Monday, and let's discuss this further. Maybe we can do this together.'

'Done, I'll speak to you on Monday. Have a great weekend!'

*This was another life-changing conversation.*

Just a few minutes earlier, I was a CEO of a tainted professional football club. And I was holding a business plan for a sports management institute, which I created for a company that was no longer in a place to activate on the idea. Now the chairman of one of the fastest growing and most respected sports management companies in India was interested in working together to establish this institute. I did not even have to express my entire mission statement. Gaurav understood that I was not just saying words, that I was living my commitment towards this area, as sincere intention always speaks louder than words.

I called Gaurav on Monday and ended up having a multi-hour conversation about life, education, sports and how to best educate and empower youth. We had similar values, thoughts and a common approach towards sports management education. It was just a joy to speak to him. I communicated that my loyalty was with Shirish and the DSK Group, and as long as there was even the slightest chance that they would be able to come out of their current challenges and establish the institute, I would do it with them. However, if it ever became clear that this would not be possible, then I would be more than happy to explore ways to support IOT with setting it up. I was not attached to which company set up the institute and even who ran it. I was solely concerned with the fact that it happens. The more I worked on the plan, the more I realized that an industry-designed sports management institute was the need of the hour.

DSK Group's legal and financial situation did not get better, and while they did ensure that they would clear their compensation commitments, the writing was on the wall for everyone at the club to see. It was time for all of us to explore other professional opportunities. It was a devastating period for everyone associated with DSK Shivajians FC and the Liverpool FC International Academy. Even now, as I reflect on this period, I get a slight ache in my heart. It was an extraordinary project that had the potential to transform football in India, and it was a pity that we did not have the opportunity to see the plan through.

We spent the next few months wrapping up the club. It was a tremendous learning experience trying to motivate a group of professional athletes, coaches and backroom staff to complete the remaining matches during a time when salaries had completely stopped. I am so proud of everyone at the club for getting over whatever fear, anger and frustration they were going through to do what was best for the sport we all loved. I even helped a few of my colleagues find new organizations to work with. I had also signed an agreement with IOT to join as the head of new business and sports education.

## Why the Process Matters?

'I'm a great believer in luck, and I find that the harder I work, the more I have of it.'— Thomas Jefferson

Then on 14 October 2017, I soberly celebrated my last day as the CEO of DSK Shivajians FC with Avantika in Pune, and the next day, I was in Bengaluru with the senior management from IOT. We were meeting to discuss the possibility of Premier League coming on board as the first partner of the yet-to-be-named IOT sports management institute. A few months earlier, I was sitting in Panchgani with all my professional frustration, confusion and discontent, trying to figure out what to do. I was now sitting with the leadership team of the top professional football league in the world and a successful sports management company in India, discussing a sports education project that was directly in line with my new formula.

How does this happen?

Luck or being in the right place at the right time?

While these may be a part of the process, what drives it is the willingness to check in with yourself when something does not feel right and having the courage and tenacity to initiate the necessary changes. In that process, new avenues for action show up, which allows for new realities to emerge. There is no way that my mind could have ever conceived of me going from being the CEO of a professional football team to becoming the head of new business and sports education for a leading sports management agency in the way that I did. Heck, I still cannot believe it. It was only by going through the process that all these opportunities presented themselves, which led me to being present in that meeting in Bengaluru, discussing a project that would completely transform the quality of my life and the future of sports management education in India.

'You don't learn to walk by following rules. You learn by doing, and by falling over.' — Richard Branson

# 15

# Overcome Your Inner Demons

*Why Are You Not Able to Move Forward?*

'Make sure your worst enemy doesn't live between your own
two ears.' — Laird Hamilton

As you take the path to attain your dream career, always
remember that two primary dream killers are lurking in the
shadows. They are mischievous, cunning and grow in power
the more you surrender to their sneak attacks. They portray
themselves as friends, people looking out for your *best
interest* whereas, they merely want you to put an end to all
this silly talk about pursuing a dream career. Unfortunately,
these killers can never be killed. They will always be with
you on your path, and the only way to defeat them is by
acknowledging their existence and continuing your journey
relentlessly. Who are these immortal killers destined to haunt
you for the rest of eternity?

## Dream Killer #1 Fear

'Too many of us are not living our dreams because we are
living our fears.' — Suzy Kassem

Fear is the ultimate dream killer because it prevents people
from even thinking about taking the first step on a road that
has the potential to lead them to limitless joy and fulfilment.
We have all experienced fear. However, the fear that is aligned
with stepping on to your dream career path is not the same as
the one that typically shows up when you hear a loud noise in
the middle of the night or on a flight that hits a heavy patch of
turbulence. No, the fear that I am referring to is less abrupt; it
finds a way to wrap its sticky tentacles around your dreams,
goals and aspirations without you even being aware that a
creature has entered the picture.

So what is fear? It is an unpleasant emotion caused by the
threat of danger, pain or harm. It typically implies anxiety or
loss of courage. Based on my experience, most individuals face
two types of fears when stepping on to or proceeding down
their dream career path.

### Fear #1: Fear of the Unknown

'We do not have a fear of the unknown. What we fear is
giving up the known.' — Anthony de Mello

This fear prevents you from stepping into unknown terrain
or losing your identity in the world. It convinces you that it
is far safer to choose well-traversed paths so that there are
clearly marked signs and people to turn to for support along

the way. It does not care whether or not you enjoy the path or are excited about the destination; what matters to this fear is that you know exactly what lies ahead.

The fear of being unknown really kicks in when you have been working for some time and are exploring a career change. Once you are established in a job for a few years, it is easy to get used to a certain identity. The idea of replacing that identity with a new one raises all sorts of red flags and disempowering thoughts—the scariest one being, 'If you are no longer known as X, who would you be?'

Venturing into unknown territory both in terms of career exploration and personal identity can be daunting. The impact of this fear is that you feel vulnerable, exposed and worried about what scary monster is waiting to pounce on you as you move ahead. It is essential to understand that the presence of this fear means that there is something important at play. That you are on to something big. Also, to realize that while its methods may not be pleasant, this fear is trying to protect you. So try to dig and discover the nugget of wisdom hidden inside of this fear. Reflect upon what is it trying to communicate that you can carry with you on your journey? Finally, recognize that it is temporary and has no substance. Just as quickly as it arrived to disrupt your creative thoughts and feelings, it can retreat into its favourite hiding place—*your subconscious mind.*

This fear has accompanied me through my entire professional journey. I felt it when I chose to pursue a career in sports management instead of joining an accounting firm like most of my closest friends in university. I felt it when I left my job at MLS and my beloved New York City to join an advertising agency in New Delhi. I felt it when I left my dear friends at Libero Sports to run a professional football club in a small city near Mumbai. I felt it when I left the traditional sports industry to dive headfirst into the education sector. Even now, I feel this fear swirling within, desperately begging for me to give it some importance.

## Fear #2: Fear of Failure

'Failure is success if we learn from it.' — Malcolm Forbes

This fear is the part of you that is only considering the worst-case scenario. It has the unique ability to direct and produce a short film in your head where you, the lead actor, pursue your dream career pathway and fail miserably. I know that I am being extreme, but this is exactly what your mind does when it is injected with fear. It conveniently forgets that you are equipped with the ability to achieve success in areas aligned with your passion, superpower and purpose.

Before getting too deep, it is important to understand what failure is *not*.

- It is not a sign that you are not as capable as someone else.
- It is also not proof that you are unworthy of success or do not have something valuable to offer the world.

*Then what is failure?*

It is merely a sign that something did not work out as planned or expected. And, most importantly, failure is rich with learnings.

I genuinely believe that the best way to learn is by doing. Whether or not you succeed, you will learn, develop insights and grow. People rarely introspect when their lives are going well, but the second they are down in the dumps, the journals, self-help books, support groups and therapist's number suddenly present themselves. Think back to past failures or the low points in your life and list out all the ways in which you grew from those experiences. These low points are important because they are part of the process, the cycle of life.

I am not saying that you will fail if you choose to go down your dream career path. I am saying the complete opposite: you *cannot* fail. If you succeed, secure your dream jobs and are fulfilled, you will be happy. If you do not achieve your goal, you will learn priceless information about yourself and your ideal career path along the way. This will help you develop resilience and reprogramme your GPS, if required, to support your journey down the road you are traversing.

I have experienced many failures throughout my career. I completely bombed several meetings with MLS executives and presentations to US football stakeholders, thanks to the fact that being 'nervous' is my default setting. In India, I was and still am a fish out of water, which means I regularly struggle through conversations in Hindi, miss out on cultural protocols and get lost when navigating the complex world of working with government entities. This has caused me to become the butt of jokes from people inside and outside of the organizations that I have worked with over the past decade. These unpleasant, and sometimes awkward, moments only encourage me to work harder and always keep a growth mindset while operating in India.

During some very dark days when I was CEO of DSK Shivajians FC and our club's finances were frozen, there were times when I was not sure if I would be able to pay our house rent for the next month or if one of our vendors whom we owed money would come to the office and physically injure me. Worse, I would lay awake at night staring at the ceiling, wondering if another sports organization would ever hire me given my association with the situation at the club. Or if Avantika has lost respect for me for convincing her to move to a new city, away from her family, and into my unexpected professional and financial chaos. Anyone who could feel my fear, sorrow and confusion during those periods would completely understand if I just packed up my bags and moved back home to my comfort zone on the beaches of Southern California.

The beautiful phenomenon about failure is that you can transform any situation where you did not achieve the expected results into something positive through insight and action. This is possible when you objectively acknowledge that the results did not meet your target and you grieve, reflect, recalibrate and move forward. This can take moments, days, months or even years, but the key is to reflect and keep moving forward. When you look back, you realize that the new possibilities created were results of the reflection, insights and aligned action associated with the so-called failure. *Therefore, you cannot truly fail; you can only learn and access information that will guide your process.*

The final message on fears is that if you have tried everything and still cannot quiet them down, the only solution is to befriend them. Let your fears know that you are going on an experimental journey via baby steps and that you can always return to your old life if you choose. Remind your fears that you are resilient, and if you fall, you will be able to stand up, shake yourself off and get right back into the game. Just do whatever you have to do to ensure that your fears do not stop you from pursuing your dream career path with full enthusiasm.

## Dream Killer #2 Inner Critic

'Your inner critic is simply a part of you
that needs more self-love.' — Amy Leigh Mercree

The inner critic is a close cousin of fear. It is the less intense but a far more annoying member of the dream killer family. This is the part of your ego that constantly offers unsolicited commentary about its favourite subject: *you*. Its weapons of choice are disempowering statements and unpleasant bodily sensations. Like fear, its intentions are good, but methods are far from desirable or productive. Also, like fear, its favourite time to attack is when you think about or are on the path towards doing something unfamiliar or something that you deeply long for.

The inner critic will definitely join you on your dream career journey. It has most likely been with you during each step of this process, sharing its opinions about you pursuing a path towards a career in line with your passion, superpower and purpose. The thing to remember is that your inner critic wants to *protect* you. It wants you to play small. It does not want you ever to leave your comfort zone and enter a place where you may fail, be exposed or hurt yourself. It shoots out statements that will prevent you from moving forward with comments like, 'You are not good enough', or 'Nobody likes you', or 'You have no talent'. You get the point? And to make matters worse, it unleashes a fury of associated bodily sensations like sweats, stomach knots, or a rapidly beating heart to make you believe that these statements are true.

### Meet Jimbo

My inner critic is a real insecure jerk named Jimbo. He is a bully, constantly telling me that I am stupid, ugly and destined to fail at everything I attempt. He also tries very hard to make sure that I know that I am really annoying and nobody actually likes me. He has been with me since I was four years old and has accompanied me on every step of my dream career journey.

Every time that I did not receive a response to my thoughtfully crafted internship application emails and letters to MLS, he would say, 'See, I told you that you could never get a job at MLS. Why would they ever hire a nobody like you?' When I was in my internship at MLS and applied for the coordinator of fan development position, it said, 'Nobody likes you here, and you barely have any experience. There is no way that you will get this job.' When I explored the idea of resigning from MLS and moving to India, it said, 'You have a good thing at MLS. Nobody has realized that you are a talentless loser yet. Don't screw it all up to go to India. You will definitely fail and end up broke, hungry, homeless and single.'

When I was settled in India and thinking about leaving Libero Sports to join DSK Shivajians FC as their CEO, it said, 'You? A CEO? Haha! What makes you think that you can lead a football club? Stay at Libero Sports; it is safer here.' When I left DSK Shivajians FC to step into sports education, Jimbo said, 'You are a complete idiot! Why throw your whole career away to jump into a new field? You will fail, no one will attend your education programme and your whole life will be a waste.' Even now, as I write this book, my inner critic is saying, 'Nobody is going to read this book. Even if they do, they will give you a crappy review. Just give up now, and let's go watch something on Netflix.'

My friend Jimbo is the cruellest, most well-intentioned person I know. Since I am aware of Jimbo's existence and intentions, he cannot harm me or impact my choices. I know that I will not be able to change his reactions to my thoughts and decisions, but I can change my story around them and how I choose to proceed. I also know that Jimbo is a product of my 'reptilian brain', which is solely focused on my survival as well as imprints or impressions of shame developed during my childhood. He is a figment of my imagination, and I am not one to let imaginary characters determine how I live my life.

*Meet Champion*

I have another imaginary friend who has also been with me since I was four years old. His name is Champion. If given the opportunity, he can actually be louder than Jimbo. He is full of empowering statements like, 'You are talented', or 'You are worthy of limitless success', or 'You are a superstar, and people love and respect you'. Champion is a dear friend, and I lean on his support and expert guidance when I am about to make a presentation in public, start a large project or embark on a new professional adventure.

As you move forward with the process, take time to identify your inner critic. Give it a name and personality. Catalogue its disempowering statements, so they do not sneak up on you at any point. Also, identify your version of your own inner champion. Get to know one another. Let it understand how much you respect its voice and presence in your life and prove your loyalty by allowing it to be the loudest voice during periods of potential stress or transition.

It is critical to remember that even if you have done everything to quiet down your inner critic, it has a few other weapons to use against you. The first is procrastination. The inner critic will innocently convince you that you can take steps towards your dream life 'later' or that there are other more pressing matters to attend to, like checking your social media accounts for the tenth time or clipping your toenails. The key to overcoming procrastination is to know that it is a lie. Not doing the primary activity will not make you feel better!

The second weapon the inner critic will use against you is telling you that you have no time or energy. Do not fall for it. You do have time if you are taking steps to live a life of joy and professional fulfilment is made a priority instead of something you squeeze into your schedule. Also, it is vital to develop a sense of boundaries so that you can say 'No' to requests if required and create space to focus on what truly matters to you.

When it comes to low energy, this can be a hindrance if you allow it to be, as energy is essential to moving along the dream career path. To ensure that you can fight the battle against the low energy monster, I recommend taking basic steps like getting proper sleep, maintaining a healthy diet and practising self-care techniques like meditation, deep breathing, regular exercise or going for walks amidst nature. It is pretty simple. Just figure out what nourishes you and provides you with clean, healthy energy and add more of these practices into your daily life.

These fears impact every human being on the planet. Thus, their appearance in your life is not a unique phenomenon. Pursuing your dream career will get messy from time to time. It is okay, do not panic or change your course of action. Understand that everyone goes through it, and the key is to be kind and compassionate towards yourself, especially during these phases. Also, I recommend spending time researching on these silent killers and the ways to manage them, as there are excellent literature and videos on these topics produced by some of the world's leading mental health experts. The more you know about them, the less they can harm you.

Your fears and the inner critic are immortal, and they can paralyse or debilitate you if you give them power. The best thing to do is acknowledge their existence; tap into your higher intelligence or inner champion; engage in practices that relax and refresh your mind, body and spirit; and get back to the dream career process work. Doing the work is the way, the only way, to reach your goals and objectives. You must take steps forward and do whatever you have to do to ensure that you do not indulge your fear or inner critic for too long, or they will definitely, 100 per cent, kill any progress you want to make towards your dreams, goals and aspirations.

I can say with complete confidence that I would not have lived a fulfilled professional life if I had given in to my fears and my inner critic. I hope that this chapter helps you to one day declare the same.

'All change is hard at first, messy in the middle and gorgeous at the end.' — Robin Sharma

# 16

# Find Your Career Bliss

*Are You Worthy of a Career That Will Bring You Fulfilment?*

## Discovering Dad's Superpower

The year was 2008.

It was Dad's retirement party. We were celebrating the fact that he had completed twenty-two years working at Hyundai Motor America and forty-four years serving some of the biggest brands as an engineer in the automobile industry. Our home was full of people. Dad's former colleagues, family members and friends from all walks of his life were present. They were happy to drink to the fact that Dad will finally be 'slowing down' after spending nearly half a century of his life working his butt off so that the world could have better cars. I was also thrilled that he was finally retiring though a part of me knew that it will take something monumental for my 'Type A' father to relax during the retirement phase of his life.

A few days before the party, I was unsure about what I could give Dad as a retirement gift because he was not the easiest person to shop for. As I thought back through my childhood to reconnect with what used to make him truly happy, an image suddenly popped in my mind: We are sitting as a family of four at our small circular table in our kitchen. Dad had finished his dinner and was drawing a landscape picture on a napkin. He was relaxed, smiling and the tense veins that typically popped out of his forehead had disappeared. I glanced at the drawing, and it was beautiful. A lush forest with an expansive mountain range in the background. Then Dad, who saw me looking, quickly crumbled the napkin and went back to sitting silently and thinking as the tense veins reappeared on his forehead.

As I continued reflecting, I realized that this was not a one-time occurrence. There were many dinners where Dad would finish his meal early and stealthily draw on any available napkin. I also remembered that when we hired interior designers to beautify our home, Dad would end up drawing sketches of what he wanted which were much better than the work the designers could do.

So, I headed to the nearest art supplies store, bought paints, a canvas and a gift certificate worth $500 that included the opportunity to take painting classes with experts in the field.

At the farewell party, Dad was opening his gifts, laughing at the cards, T-shirts and mugs with jokes printed on them like, 'I thought I'd retired, but now I just work for my wife'. Then he got to my gift, unwrapped the canvas and paints and read the card which said that he had $500 to spend at the local art supplies store. He went silent, and I was waiting for him to cry, hug me and say, 'Thank you, son, this is the best gift anyone has ever given me. You truly understand me. I love you.' Instead, he said, 'I hope you kept the receipt as I may need to return this.' Everyone at the party broke out into drunken laughter, as he moved on to the next present.

Once the house emptied of guests, my parents, Paras and I sat in our family room, indulging in a nightcap and chatting.

I said, 'Dad, I just have one request. One day next week, set up the canvas on an easel, turn on relaxing music and just paint.'

'I've never painted in my life, why would I start when I'm sixty-six years old?'

'Because I've spent my childhood watching you draw beautiful landscapes on napkins, and those times were some of the most relaxed I've ever seen you.'

'Really? Those were just silly drawings to pass the time after dinner.'

'Just try, if you don't like it, you can give the paint supplies away.'

'Sure, I'll try.'

Dad went a step further. He took a beginner's art class and then an intermediate one and started painting daily for hours. Within one month, he had already painted five beautiful landscapes and let go of the daily evening cocktail that helped him relax after a full day of intense work at Hyundai. I would speak to him on the phone from New York during those days, and he sounded like someone who was living his best life, and Mom was over the moon as she had not seen him this way in decades. Dad was spending time with my cousin, Kushal, who was also into painting, and they would bond over painting styles and colour palettes instead of the usual stock market and family gossip. It was a complete transformation, and I decided to fly back to California to see it first-hand.

Dad picked me up from the airport, and we talked about his love for painting the entire way down to our home. Like a child, he was proud of and excited to share his projects with his loved ones. When I entered my home, I saw eight landscape paintings displayed on our fireplace. I just kept staring at them in complete shock and surprise. They were beautiful, worthy of being in any art gallery. It was unbelievable that in just over a month, my father had become a full-fledged artist, and, more than that, he genuinely seemed happy.

I could not stop thinking about Dad and the joy exuding within and through him, thanks to his new-found love for painting. I never saw him this happy during his career as an automotive engineer, even though he loved cars and was respected in his field. He worked diligently each day but never came home bubbling with joy or sincerely interested in sharing his work. He mainly returned from the office in tense silence and would retreat to his computer and drown himself in the stock market and an evening cocktail. We rarely got to experience this happy-go-lucky childlike person who was bouncing around the house with his paint set unless maybe if we were on a family trip or hosting a party.

I was determined to examine this at a deeper level and sat with my father to discuss his formula one evening. We went through the self-reflection questions and came up with the following formula for Dad:

[(Passion: Cars) + (Superpower: Picturing something in his mind and drawing it exactly as it is)] x Purpose: Fill the world with the best-looking and most efficient automobiles.

- Possible Dream Jobs:
    - Automotive designer
    - Design consultant for automobile companies
    - Automotive engineer—with a focus on design

It was so clear, Dad's career always included two out of three of his elements. He always worked with cars and had the opportunity to fill the world with the best-looking and most efficient automobiles; however, he did not have the chance to apply his ability to picture something in his mind and draw it exactly as it is. He was always in the product development department, so most of his time at work was analyzing the various functional elements of automobiles and determining how to build more efficient and sustainable cars *when his heart was yearning to design them*. This was one of the primary reasons he always liked his job but was rarely fulfilled by it.

I could not help but ask him, 'Dad, did you ever love your job?'

'I'm not sure; I liked cars and always felt grateful that I had a job and could provide for our family.'

'That's great and we appreciate it. But did you ever *love* your job?'

'No, I guess I never really loved my job.'

'How come you started working in the product development department early in your career?'

'Because I graduated with my master's in Automotive Engineering from Oklahoma State University and saw a job posting at Ford for a position in the product development department. I applied, got hired and then never really thought about switching departments.'

'Do you think you would have enjoyed being an automotive designer instead of working in the product development department?'

(Dad lighting up.)

'Yes, actually, I always envied my colleagues who would get to manually draw and then eventually use computers to design the next models of cars.'

'Do you think that you would have excelled at being an automotive designer?'

'Yes, now that I realize how good I am with drawing and given my love for cars, I feel that I would have been a great automotive designer. And I would have enjoyed the work as well.'

Without even knowing it, Dad was starting to draft his mission statement, just forty years too late. I sat up at night, imagining what my father's 100,000 hours could have been like if he had realized that his superpower was accurately drawing what was on his mind. Maybe he would have held off on accepting a position with the product development team at Ford and pursued positions that involved product design. Or possibly taken the job with Ford and eventually pivoted to work with the design team. And how would that have impacted his growth in his field and his professional fulfilment? And how would that have affected his mental and physical health as well as our experience of living with him?

So many thoughts ran through my head and, with them, a clear message that I must help others discover their formulae so that they do not miss out on the opportunity to fully enjoy their lives. This conversation and the questions that arose afterward led me to write this book.

## How to Find Your Career Bliss

I have seen this situation many times in the past. Someone jumps into a job or career pathway and trudges forward, not knowing if they are on the correct stream or even flowing in the right direction.

- Do not make this mistake and miss out on the opportunity to experience career bliss.
- Do not allow feelings of job dissatisfaction to linger for too long without checking in with yourself and taking some action.

- Do not wait until you are retired to feel the type of relaxed joy you could have experienced during your career.

It does take self-reflection. It does take working with your formula. It does include taking S-M-A-R-T steps. It does take some level of courage and patience as well. I know that, in 2003, if I joined MLS in a department that did not align with my formula, I may not have experienced the success and fulfilment that I did.

## What Do You Want?

- A job?
- Professional security?
- A salary?

There is nothing wrong with that. We all want these. However, there is something wrong with not believing that you are worthy of a career that will bring you fulfilment. There is something amiss with not doing the inner work required to find out what truly makes you happy, what you are good at and how you want to serve the world. There is something off about allowing your family, your community, your educational institutes or your pesky mind to pressure you into choosing a path that may not lead to the most fulfilling way to spend your 100,000 hours.

Your career is not a jail where you are 'imprisoned' for the rest of your life.

## *How to be Free?*

Keep checking in with yourself and see if all three elements of your formula are in line with what you are doing professionally and make adjustments if and when required. It is as simple as that.

Our world is big; it needs many services and continues to expand on a day-to-day basis. There will always be a place for someone with your formula to serve, as long as you are clear on how you want to show up in the world. So, do not fall into the trap caused by impatience, fear, resignation or laziness to do the inner work. It is not worth it. Once you are in the trap, it is easy to flip on the switch of justification to numb the discontent resulting from not having your career(s) as a natural extension of yourself. If you are in that space, do what you need to shift into a heart-set of possibility and take steps to design your dream career in a way that feels right for you.

'You are never given a dream without also being given the power to make it come true. You will have to work for it, however.' — Richard Bach

# 17

# Begin Your Dream Career Journey

*Are You Ready?*

It was 20 December 2019.

I was standing on a stage that was built on a football pitch in Powai. Behind me was a gorgeous view of Mumbai with Powai Lake in the foreground. Dressed in a traditional cap and gown meant for graduation ceremonies, I took a deep breath and looked up. In front of me was our first batch of graduating students from the Global Institute of Sports Business (GISB), India's first industry-designed and internationally certified sports management institute, a project that I had somehow taken from concept to reality. The gathering also included their proud parents, leaders from the Indian sports industry and some of the country's top self-development facilitators. My gorgeous, expressive arts therapist wife was present as well.

The setting was just perfect. It reflected everything important to me: family, football, education, self-development, community and, of course, India. At that moment, I was in awe, completely mesmerized by the magic of the universe, the power of manifestation and one's ability to make the impossible possible. GISB was a natural extension of myself, a consolidation of all my experiences, learnings and global networks and happened to be the need of the hour for India to produce the next generation of global sports industry leaders.

Our students go through months of self-development work to build a solid foundation that is necessary in life, especially when trying to create change in a highly dynamic industry like sports. The faculty is made up of some of the finest professionals from around the world. As a part of the programme, our students have the opportunity to travel to England to spend time learning about the business of sport from Premier League and Premier League club officials. Finally, the programme is certified by the University of Massachusetts, Amherst, which has the topmost ranked Sports Management programme in the world and the alma mater of my first boss at MLS and mentor David Wright in addition to several other global sports industry peers. Thanks to GISB, I was able to connect the worlds of sports and education while empowering individuals to create an impactful and fulfilling career pathway for themselves.

A single tear formed in my left eye and trickled down my cheek. For the first time in my life, words did not do justice to how I felt. My heart was full, I was grateful and I thanked everyone for believing in themselves and in the power of sports to transform lives. I also thank our incredible management team for partnering with me to build and run India's best sports management institute. I finally thank Will Norton of the University of Massachusetts for believing in this project and bringing global best practices in sports education to India. I left the podium to gracious applause and walked back to my seat next to Gaurav Modwel, the chairman of India On Track and chancellor of GISB, without whom this project would not have come to fruition.

I took another breath and then took it all in: My journey from Jim's office twenty-five years earlier, where I planted the seed that I would work in football; to the conversation with Tom Dell at the Hyundai office; to the thrill of running my first football camp; to speaking to the MLS receptionist and Mark Noonan on the phone across the street from the MLS league office; to getting offered my first dream job at MLS; to the wake-up moment inside the Kashipura village home; to the conversations with Sukhvinder about moving to India and then flying over to New Delhi and struggling for years both personally and professionally, trying to find my feet in this new land; to all the ups and downs and self-reflection sessions in Prospect Park, Lodhi Gardens, Panchgani, that all led to this very moment. I smiled, knowing that it was all worth it. Not just the destination, the journey was exciting, adventurous and, most importantly, incredibly fulfilling.

I have had the opportunity to live a dream life and have done it without any special strengths beyond my superpower. I am someone who chose to enjoy most of my 100,000 hours of professional life and took the necessary steps no matter what internal or external pressures surfaced along the way. Anyone can do this. *You can.* Choose a path that is a natural extension of yourself.

The beauty is that no one knows where this path may eventually lead. When I was sitting in Jim's office or during my early years at MLS, I would have laughed if someone were to tell me that I would be living in Mumbai and working in sports management education. But this is where my formula led me, and I could not be happier. Your path can lead you to stay in your hometown, lead you to another state or country, keep you in the same company your whole life, make you shift to different organizations or industries, or have you start your own firm.

This will all only become clear as you go through the process. You may feel more 'secure' sticking with something you know or understand versus taking steps towards the unknown. But it is riskier to stay in a situation where you are pretty certain that you will not enjoy your 100,000 hours instead of taking steps in a direction where those hours could feel more enjoyable. If you believe in your passion, superpower and purpose, you will ultimately do well in your chosen career(s).

The only way all this can be a reality is to start the process, always be willing to go within yourself and see if you are aligned with your professional scope of work.

That is it. You have the power to create anything you want for yourself and your life. If you have read until this point, I wholeheartedly believe that you are destined to always be on the pathway to your dream career. Stay committed to generate your own bliss. Experience pure, unadulterated joy through your vocation so that you can share it with your loved ones.

Thank you for allowing me to further my mission of empowering individuals to pursue their dream career(s) so that the world can always be full of happy and fulfilled people. This is my dream career story. Now I invite you to live and share your own.

# Acknowledgements

Writing this book allowed me to reflect on my life and all the individuals that have contributed to my professional journey. I am eternally grateful to my parents for their love, support and sacrifice. They are truly at the source of everything good that has happened in my life.

To my elder brother, Paras, for always supporting and encouraging my passions and generously allowing me to share his story with the readers.

To my incredible wife, Avantika, for her love and companionship, and patience while I bombarded her with thoughts, questions, insights and doubts about this book in between her client therapy sessions. Also, for stepping way out of her comfort zone, and letting me include details of her professional journey in the book.

I am blessed to have several mentors and guides in my life who believed in me even when I did not always believe in myself: Sunil Gulati, David Wright, Geoff Hayes, Kathy Carter, Marco Liceaga, Tarun Chaudhry, Sukhvinder Singh, Alex Eu, Arvind Narayan, Eddie Rock, Shirish Kulkarni, Gaurav Modwel and Vivek Sethia. I would like to acknowledge some of my amazing teammates with whom I have had the pleasure of building organizations and programmes with over the years: Jerome Rankine, James Morris, Pepe Galván, Jesse Perl, Randeep Baruah, Sweekar Kapoor, Karan Jindal, Raunak Balasubramanian, Abhishek Wakankar, Nula Kohringam, Sahil Bhat, Reuben Borah, Pinky Gandhi, Saurabh Mehta, Nimisha Tailor, Rajashree Bhattacharyya, Maher Ranina, Varun Koli, Khush Jajoo, Pratik Sonawane, Raina Michael, Sandesh Pandav, Miti Doshi and Dayanand Birajdar.

Thank you Ajay Mago, publisher of Om Books International, for publishing my story and my unique philosophy for creating a fulfilling career. My editor Jyotsna Mehta for brilliantly editing this book. Special mention to OBI's chief editor Shantanu Ray Chaudhuri, one of the best editors in the business, for being my champion. The team at OBI has been supportive in every step of the way.

Also, my deep gratitude to the team at The Book Bakers, led by the ever-supportive and dynamic literary agent Suhail Mathur, for helping me navigate the world of publishing.

A big thank you to my super talented sister-in-law, Akanksha Malhautra, for her keen eye for detail and candid feedback while I was writing this book. I also thank my dear friend Marian Brehmer for tapping into his wealth of experience as a journalist to strengthen the text.

I wrote the majority of this book during the first year of the pandemic when the world was in lockdown. However, I was fortunate to spend this time quarantining at a dear friend's beautiful holiday home located in the hills a few hours' drive from Mumbai. It turned out to be the perfect environment to write a book, all made possible thanks to my lovely soul sister Megha Modi and her generous parents, Ramesh and Anu Modi. The caretakers of the home, Ramesh and Kavita, as well as their fun-loving children Meghna and Prachi and dogs Shanti and Shantam, who serendipitously showed up while we were staying there, made writing this book a joyful experience.

Finally, my gratitude and blessings to you, the reader. I acknowledge you for choosing to read this book on creating a dream career and playing your part in bringing more happiness into the world.